CITY WORKS | 7

CITY WORKS | 7

The City College of New York
Bernard and Anne Spitzer School of Architecture

Student Work 2012-2013

Edited by Nandini Bagchee & Bradley Horn
Foreword by George Ranalli

OSCAR RIERA OJEDA
PUBLISHERS

MESSAGE FROM THE DEAN

CONTENTS

The problems faced by the infrastructure of cities and questions of resilience proved fertile ground for learning to innovate in design studios across the board this past academic year. The landscape architecture program explored the shoreline of New York in the wake of hurricane Sandy and hosted the timely conference Waterproofing New York in 2013. In a parallel exploration of the water's edge, urban design studios explored the development of ports in Istanbul and Tianjin. Recognizing the necessity of forming strong relationships to face civic challenges, studio coordinators also fostered a series of partnerships with local institutions. The architecture students of the first year masters and the third year undergraduate programs found a client in the Harlem School of the Arts. The fourth year undergraduate design studio proposed alternative programs on a problematic site for the Atlantic Avenue Building Improvement Development in Brooklyn. This seventh issue of City Works represents the commitment of the students and faculty at the Spitzer School of Architecture to a continued engagement with social and environmental sustenance within the city.

It has been a privilege for me to co-edit this volume of city works with Bradley Horn. We appreciate the efforts of Salvatore Cosenza and Jennifer Ewald for their thoughtful and diligent work in producing this book. We would like to extend our thanks to our publisher, Oscar Reira Ojeda whose graphic sensibility and precision brings cohesion to this work. The evocative cover photographs of our colleague, Albert Vecerka provide a graceful frame for the creative efforts and undertakings of the faculty, staff and students at the school. We thank them all for their contribution.

Nandini Bagchee, Co-editor

INTRODUCTION

2012–13 was a remarkable year for the Spitzer School of Architecture, with two architects connected with the school receiving high honors. Michael Sorkin, Distinguished Professor at Spitzer, was awarded the Design Mind award from the Smithsonian's Cooper-Hewitt National Design Museum, while James Wines, subject of a yearlong exhibit here, received Cooper-Hewitt's Lifetime Achievement award.

James Wines's "A Line Around an Idea" was our gallery's featured exhibit this year, with approximately eighty five original drawings sumptuously illustrating his remarkable design ethos. One of the show's most dramatic aspects was a sketch of Jim's enlarged to enormous size, reproduced onto a durable surface, and placed on the floor of the gallery. The drawing could be viewed from any point in the school having a view down into the gallery. A film of Jim making an original watercolor drawing, which ran at the entry to the gallery, demonstrated his exceptional facility with pen, ink, and wash in the expression of his vision. The architectural ideas embedded in the show were all seminal; one could see how far ahead his vision was at every point in his career.

In October 2012 the Franklin D. Roosevelt Four Freedoms Park opened. Designed by Louis I. Kahn in the early 1970s, the project laid unfinished for over forty years, but money was finally secured and the project came to life on the southern tip of Roosevelt Island. It has provoked a remarkable range of positive critiques around the globe. We offered our spring lecture series to deepen our understanding of Kahn's work, design methodology, and uncanny awareness of the metaphysics of institutions and their meaning to society.

Lastly, this spring saw Marshall Berman give the annual Mumford Lecture to a large crowd in Shepard Hall. Berman, in his typical fashion, wove a web of urban history, folklore, and transformation that was both spellbinding and illuminating. His scintillating presentation on his beloved Bronx displayed a deep knowledge of how specific elements, such as the Cross Bronx Expressway, caused upheavals to the previously tranquil neighborhood.

As we reveled in Marshall's brilliance, no one foresaw that this would be one of his last lectures. Only a few months later, on September 11, he passed away suddenly. He was a gifted teacher, wonderful colleague, and remarkable thinker, and wove his intellectual spell weekly with Spitzer students every spring. His warm presence will be sorely missed by all students and faculty that knew him and enjoyed his spectacular intellectual gifts.

George Ranalli, Dean

BACHELOR OF ARCHITECTURE

Semester 1 14
Semester 2 24
Semester 3 34
Semester 4 44
Semester 5 54
Semester 6 64
Semester 7 74
Semester 8 84
Comprehensive Design 94

MASTER OF ARCHITECTURE

Semester 1 108
Semester 2 114
Semester 3 120
Semester 4 126
Semester 5 132
Semester 6 138

MASTER OF URBAN DESIGN 146

MASTER OF LANDSCAPE ARCHITECTURE

Semester 1 154
Semester 2 158
Semester 3 164
Semester 4 170
Semester 5 176
Thesis 180

MASTER OF SCIENCE
SUSTAINABILITY IN THE URBAN ENVIRONMENT 186

VISUAL STUDIES 196

DAVID WERBER TRAVELING FELLOWSHIP IN BARCELONA 206
SPITZER TRAVEL GRANT 2012 212

LECTURE & EVENTS 2012 - 2013 218

FACULTY & STAFF 238

BACH

OF ARCHITECTURE

ELOR

1st SEMESTER DESIGN

FACULTY
Johanna Dickson / David Judelson /
Fran Leadon / Suzan Wines

The fall semester focuses on three projects exploring the basics of design: the making of architectural space through simple repetitive exercises that gradually become more complex.

The sequence of exercises begins with threshold, introducing basic drafting skills, free hand sketching and diagramming, and model making in wood using a structural system of planes and corners that describe space, time, gravity, sequence, and transition. Threshold then becomes directional, yielding a path through a landscape of the student's own invention. Scale is introduced, and the program allows a close examination of the relationships of site and structure, space and time. Land is explored as tectonic pieces rather than a continuous, uninterrupted sheet. The relationship between built space and carved space is explored in great detail. The final project, place, allows the students to focus on a detailed spatial moment extracted from their path project.

The human figure at rest and in motion is examined in detail as a way of determining the spatial relationships of the program. Scale, sun orientation, materials, and structural systems are examined in more detail, culminating in a large-scale model and drawings.

Fran Leadon
First Year Design Coordinator

Leanne Zick
DAVID JUDELSON, CRITIC

01

02

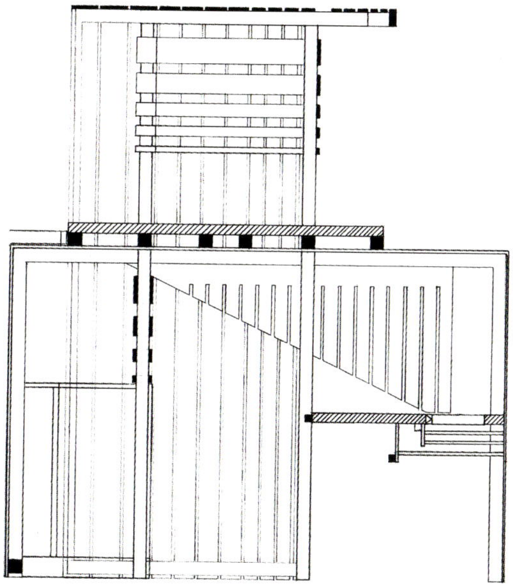
03

01 | Sivan Weizmann
02, 03 | Ashley Holmes

01

02

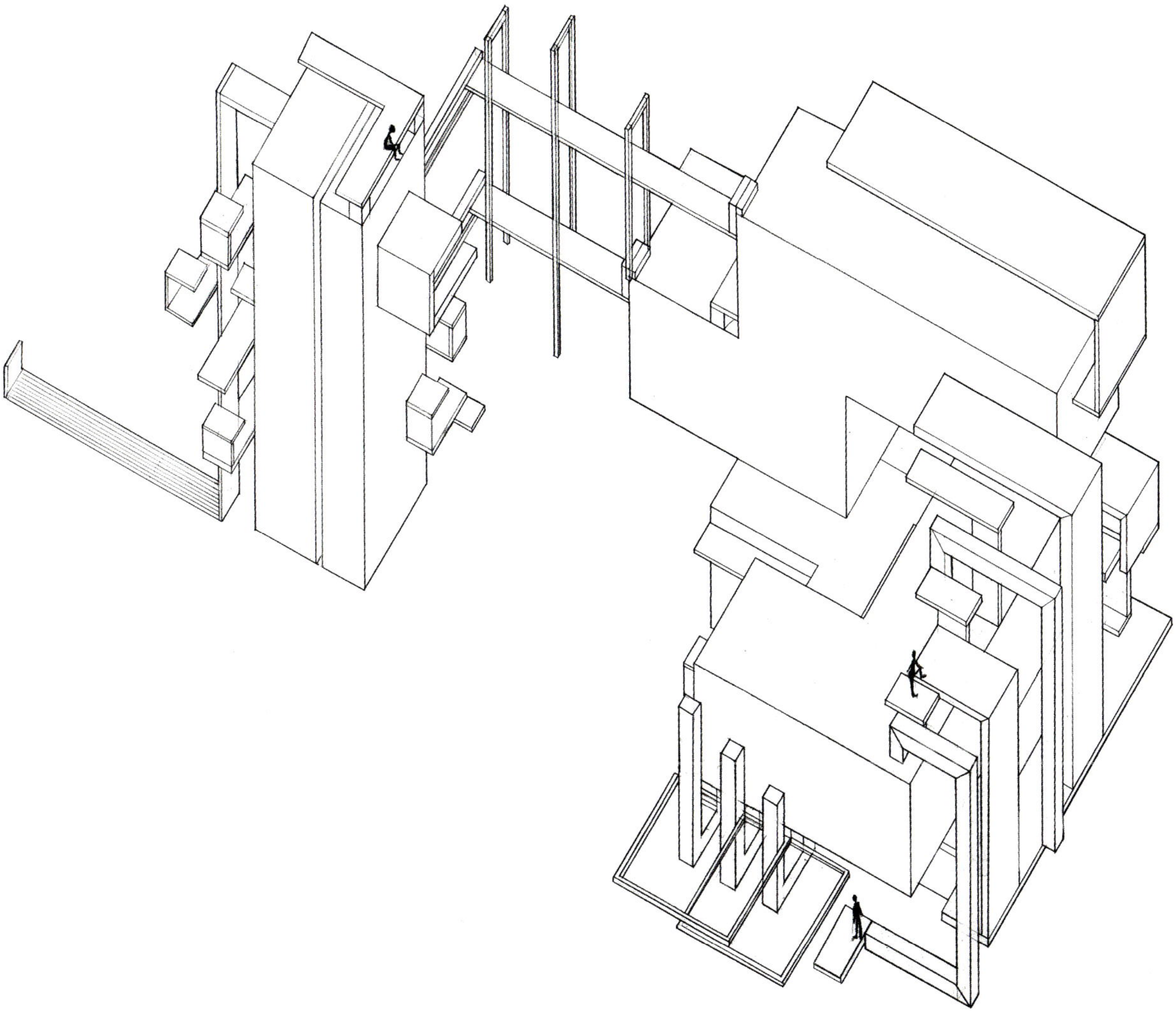

03

04

01 | Akram Hasan
02 | Christina Bien-Aime
03 | Vionna Wai
04 | Jeffrey Crowley

01

02

01 | Cynthia Yin
02 | Julian Usman / Cheuk Hui / Sunny Fok

01

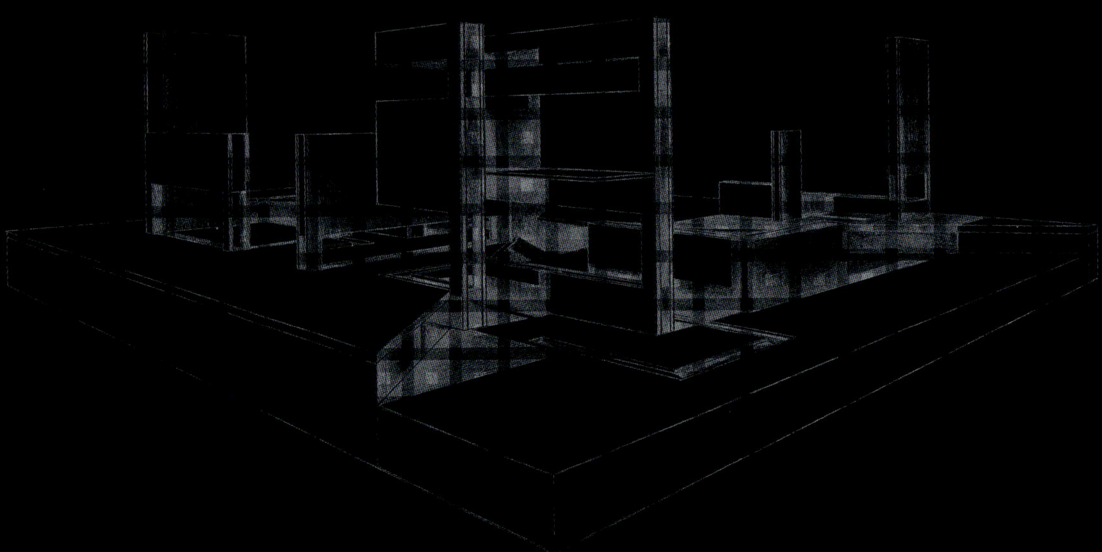

02

03

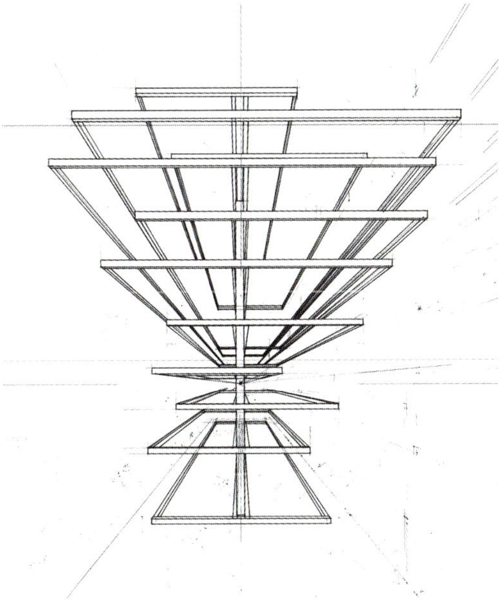

04

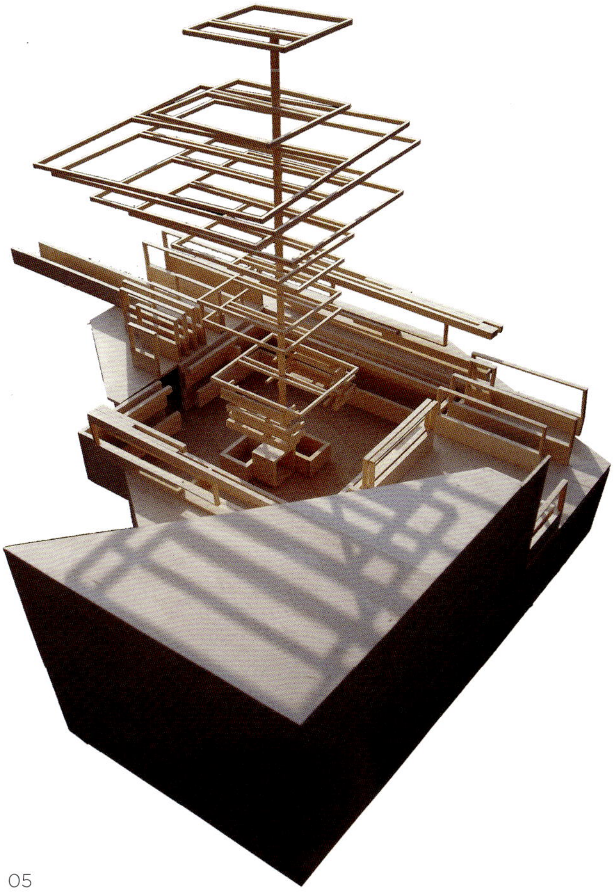

05

01, 02 | Rafiul Prodhan
03-05 | Eunice Yujung Jung

2nd SEMESTER DESIGN

FACULTY
Johanna Dickson / David Judelson /
Fran Leadon / Suzan Wines

The spring semester begins with students divided into teams for a detailed Precedent Study. Each instructor examines the work of a different architect, which in the past has included Wright, Neutra, Le Corbusier, Barragan and Kahn. Teams complete a full set of drawings and very detailed "museum-quality" models that specifically explore the buildings as spatial sequences and the relationship of the building to the landscape. Students acquire a high level of precision and craft, and work together in mutually supportive teams.

Each student then extracts a structural system from their precedent study and develops a Spatial Sequence at 1/4" = 1'-0" using the formal operations "fold, unfold, cut, stretch, and multiply." Students construct wood models of the sequence and are asked tospeculate on the open question "what is the nature of nature?" The project focuses on making space out of structure and on developing and encouraging each student's individual self-directed process and awareness of a broader context for their work.

For their final project, students are given a new site and program. Each student edits and reinterprets their Spatial Sequence project as a Weather Station, designed for one or two researchers to observe the weather and to enter and store data in record books. Each student is encouraged to define a system of gathering, sorting, editing and prioritizing data that is analogous to both the organization of spatial systems and to their own design process.

Fran Leadon
First Year Design Coordinator

Francesca Messina
SUZAN WINES, CRITIC

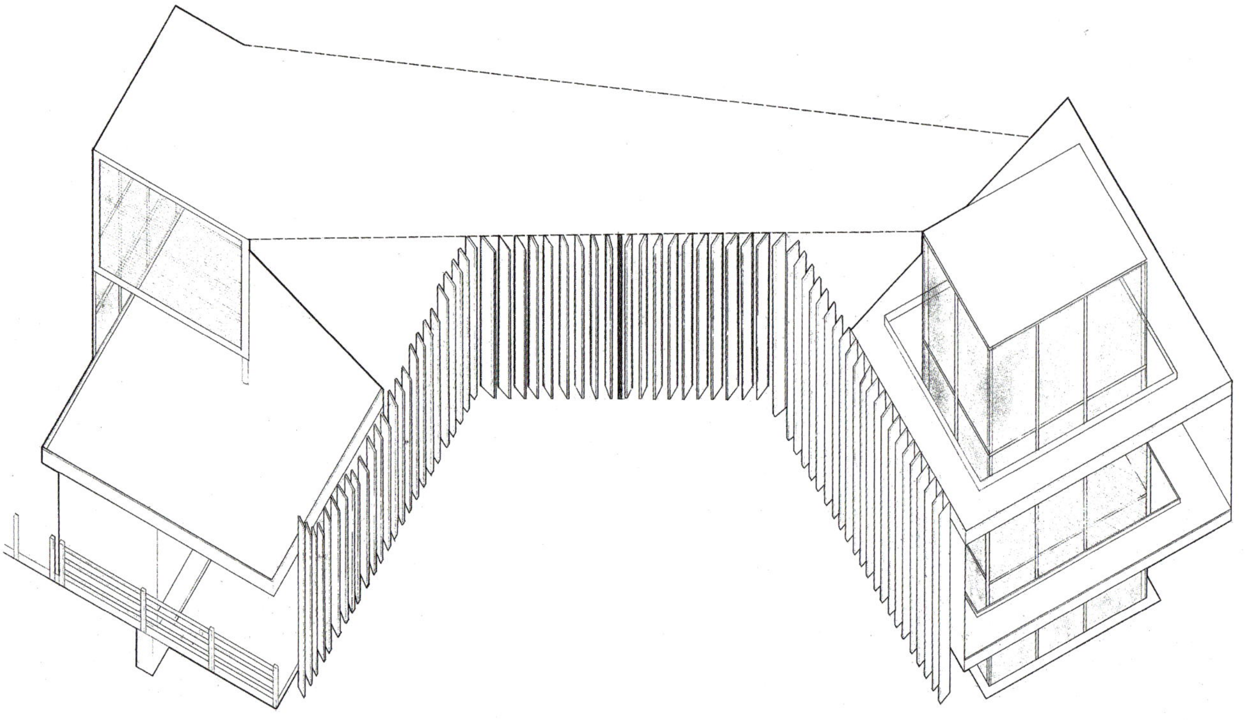

01

02

03

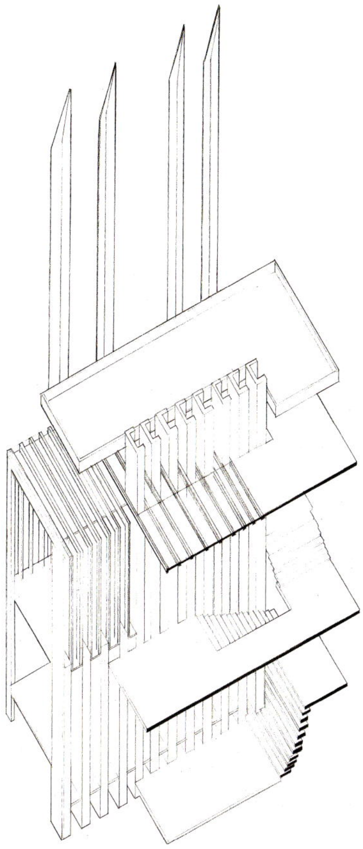

04

05

01 | Sivan Weizmann
02, 03 | Julian Usman
04, 05 | Stephania Papadopoulos

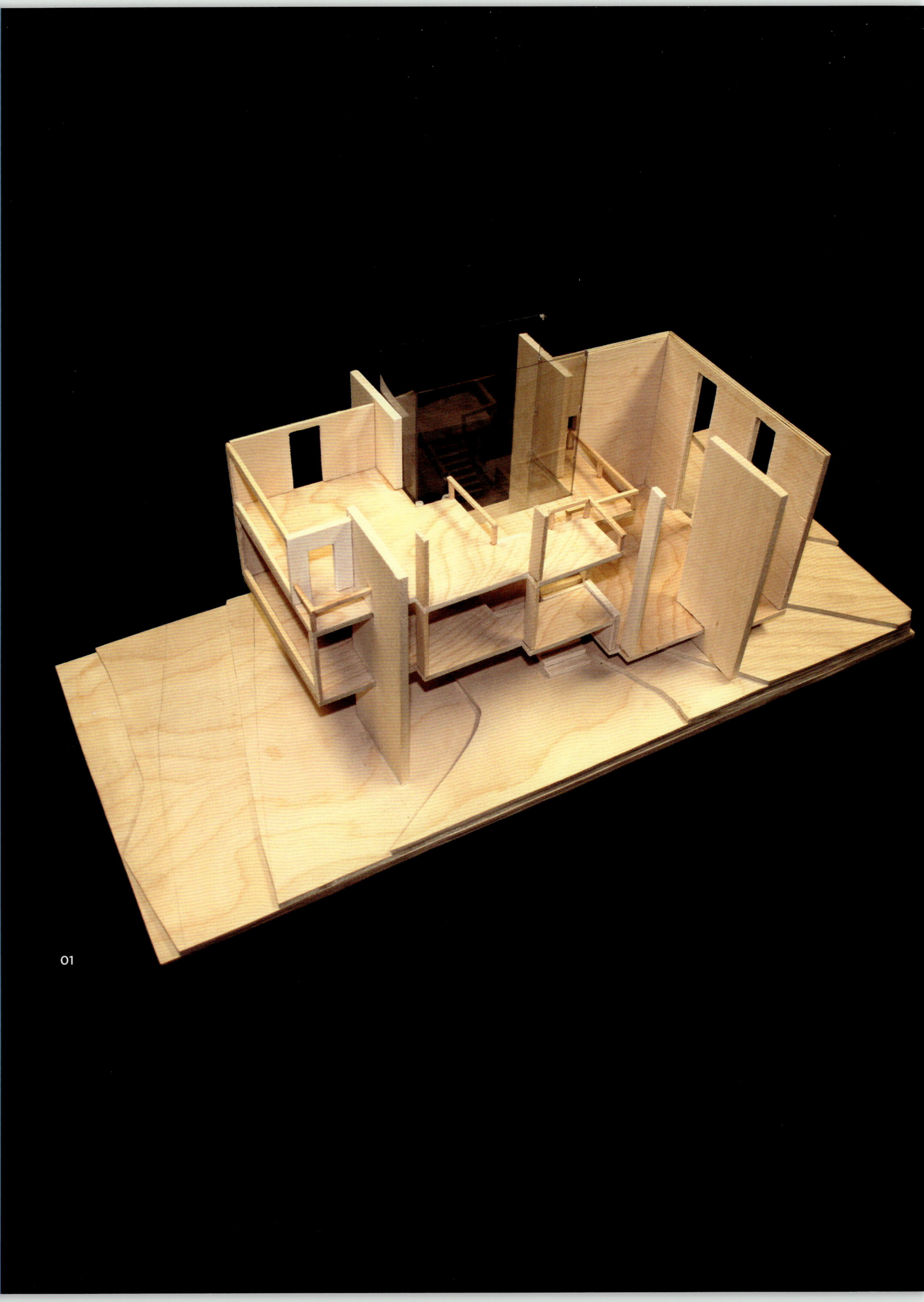

01

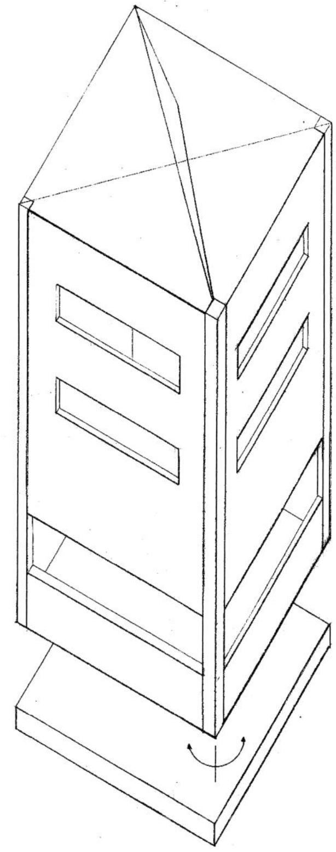

02

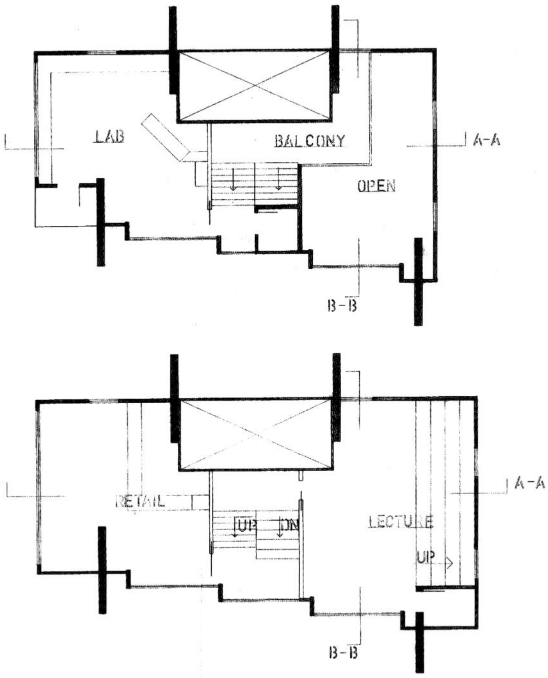

03

01-03 | Dmitriy Polyakov

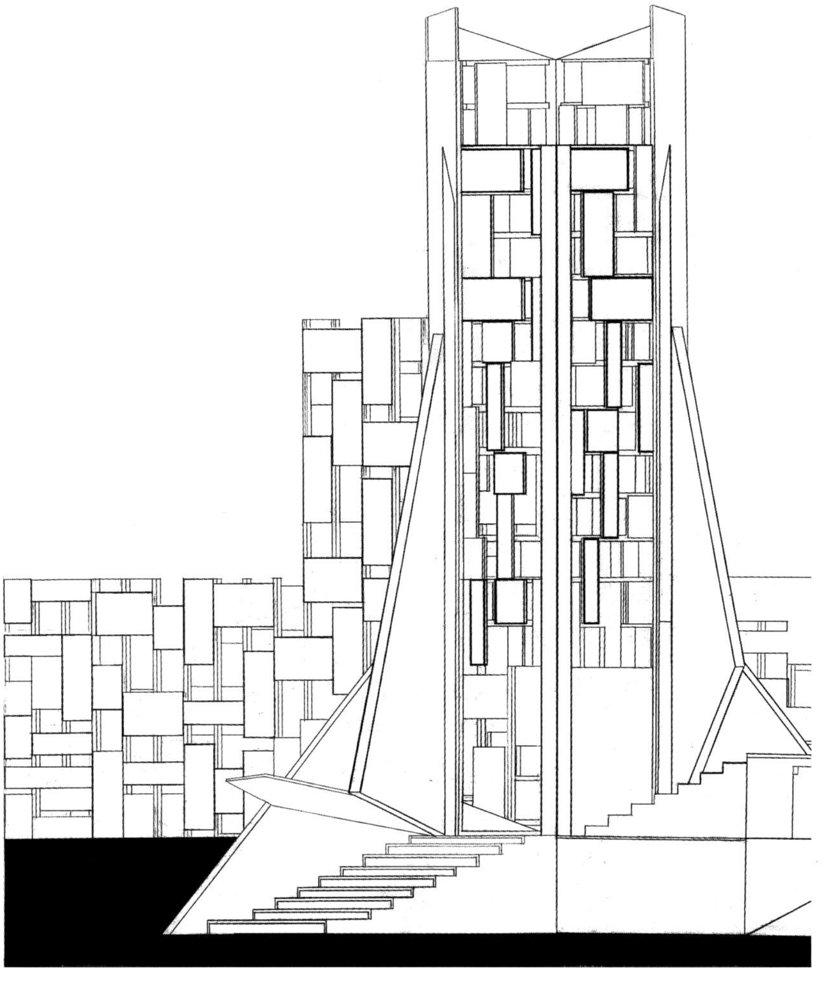

01

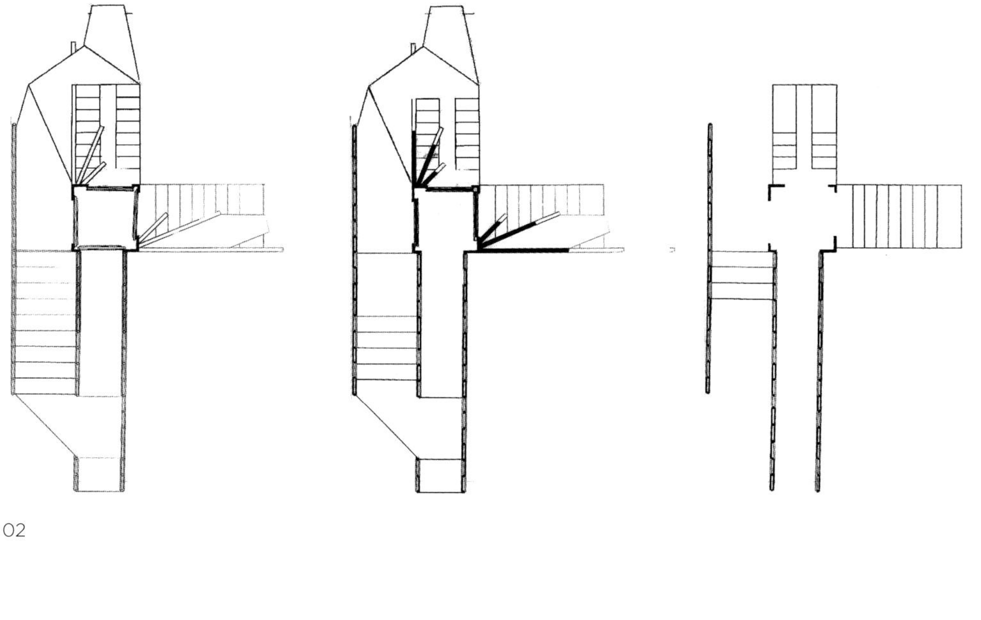

02

03

04

01, 02 | Emanuel Gjini / Rafiul Prodhan
03, 04 | Wei Ying Zhang / Shereese Trumpet

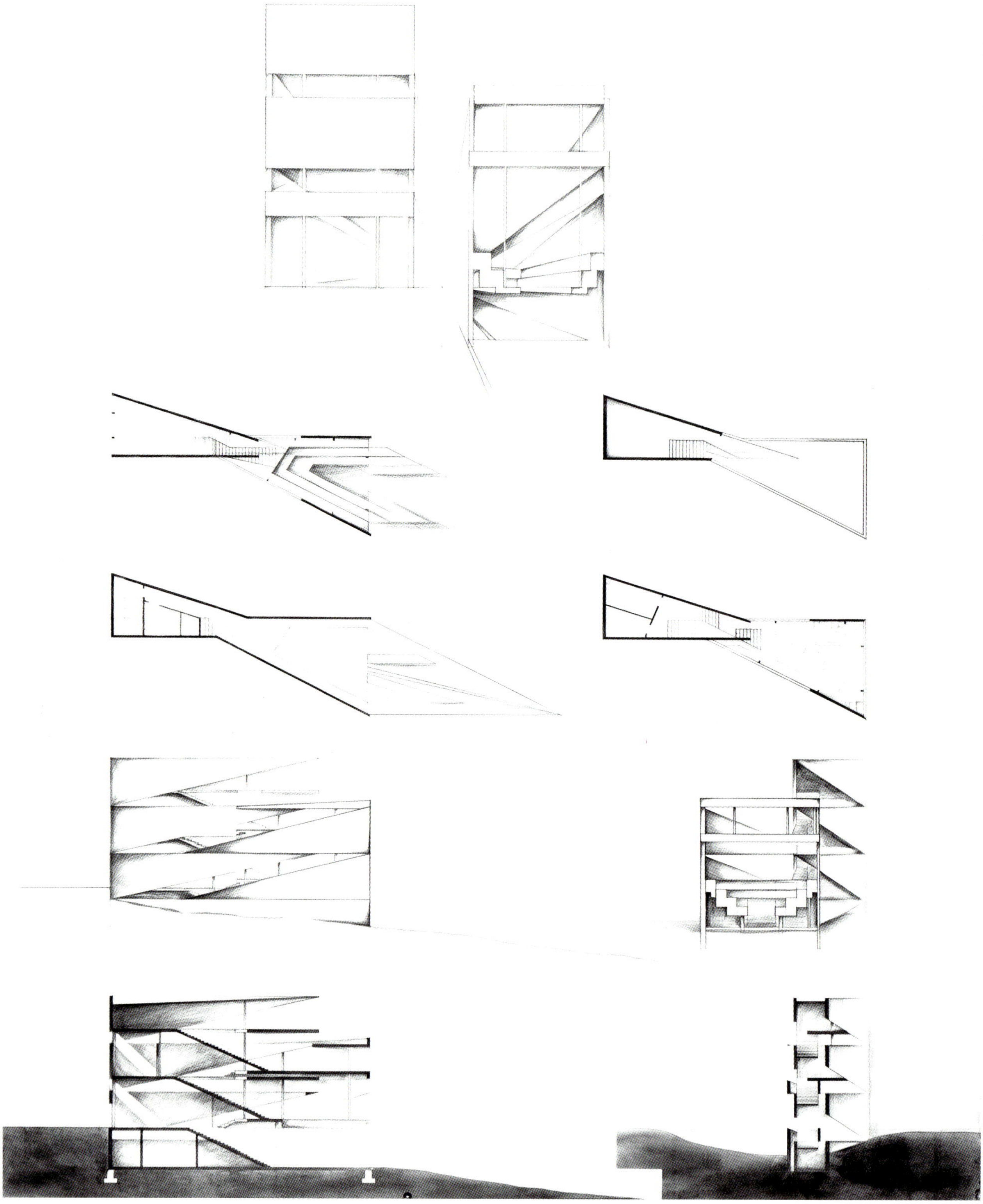

01

02

03

04

01 | Kaitlin Faherty
02, 03 | Timur Sayfulin
04 | Francesca Messina

3rd SEMESTER DESIGN

FACULTY
Nandini Bagchee / Antonio Di Oronzo / Athanasios Haritos / Adam Hayes

In the fall of 2012, the second year students staged spontaneous performances on the sidewalks along Houston Street in lower Manhattan. These actions interrupted the regular activity along a busy thoroughfare and allowed the students to experience the space of a New York sidewalk from a different perspective. Working in small groups, they documented their actions via video and later worked them into drawings of the storefronts, passersby and the built environment through an iterative process. These street performances and the representations of the sidewalk generated an understanding of the potential of a site as a place of both ephemeral and permanent occupations. The spatial analysis of the street and its many bounding conditions became fodder for the design of a compact, temporary, performance booth on a traffic island on Houston Street.

In a second exercise, this same triangular plot of land was developed into a theater to accommodate formal performances, rehearsal spaces and related workshops. Moving from the scale of the body of a performer to investigate a series of civic relationships between an audience and the city allowed the students to speculate on the complexity of programming a communal space. Analyzing the history of an urban site from a subjective and objective vantage allowed a sense of social engagement and creative play to permeate their final theater proposals. This second year design studio aimed at creating an awareness of the city and the multiple ways in which experience can inform architecture.

Nandini Bagchee
Second Year Design Coordinator

Eliza Tan
ANTONIO DI ORONZO, CRITIC

01

02

03

04

01 | Katherine Serrano
02 | Anna Kwiatkowska
03 | James Geoghegan
04 | Amy Naranjo

01

02

03

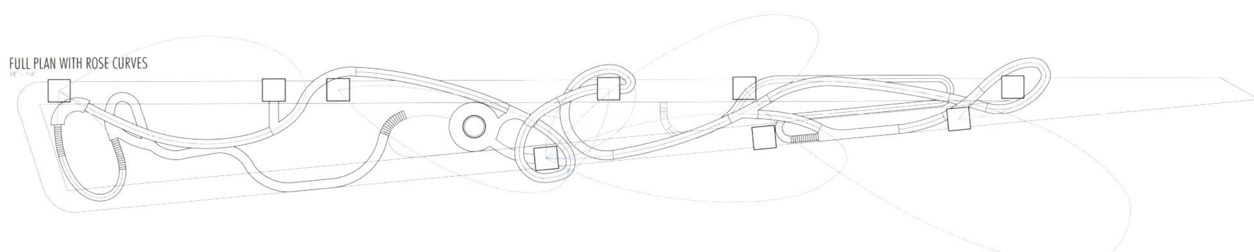

04

01, 02 | Roman Hatnyanskyy
03, 04 | Eliza Tan

01

02

03

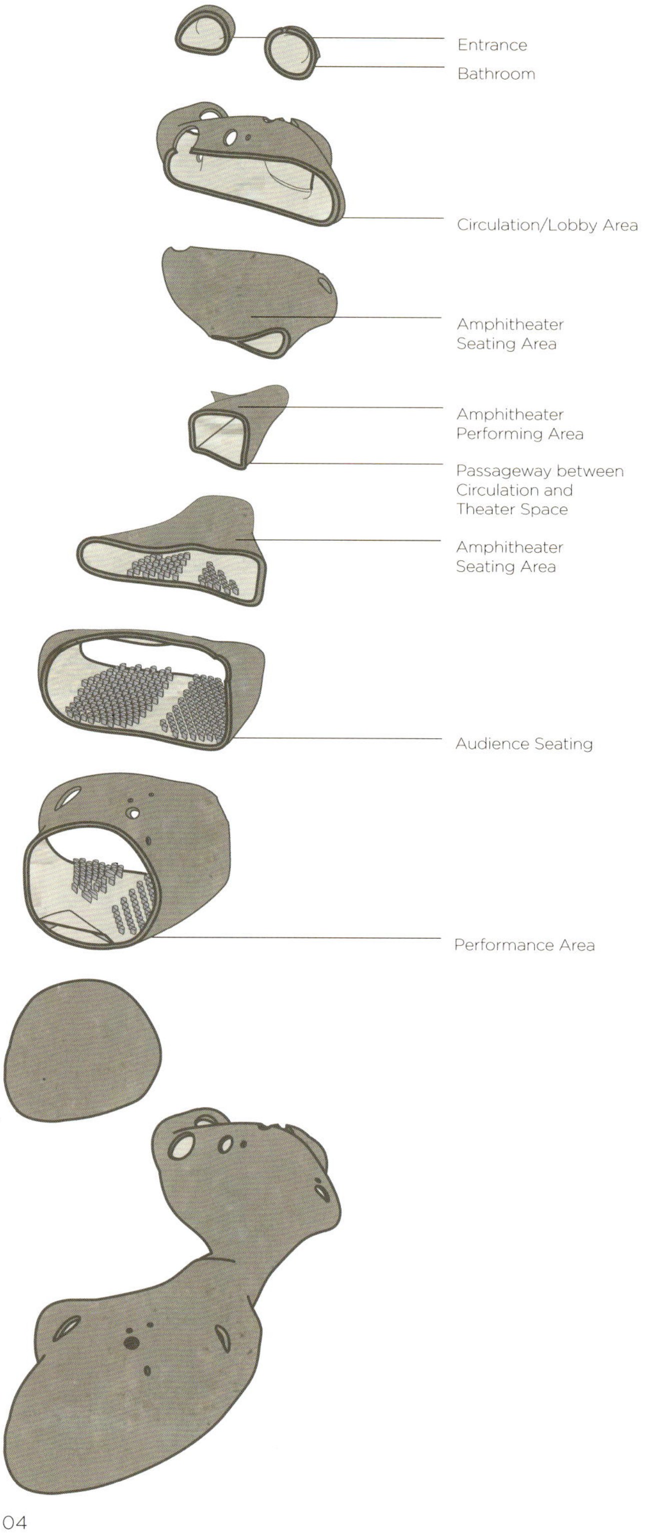
Entrance
Bathroom
Circulation/Lobby Area
Amphitheater
Seating Area
Amphitheater
Performing Area
Passageway between
Circulation and
Theater Space
Amphitheater
Seating Area
Audience Seating
Performance Area

04

05

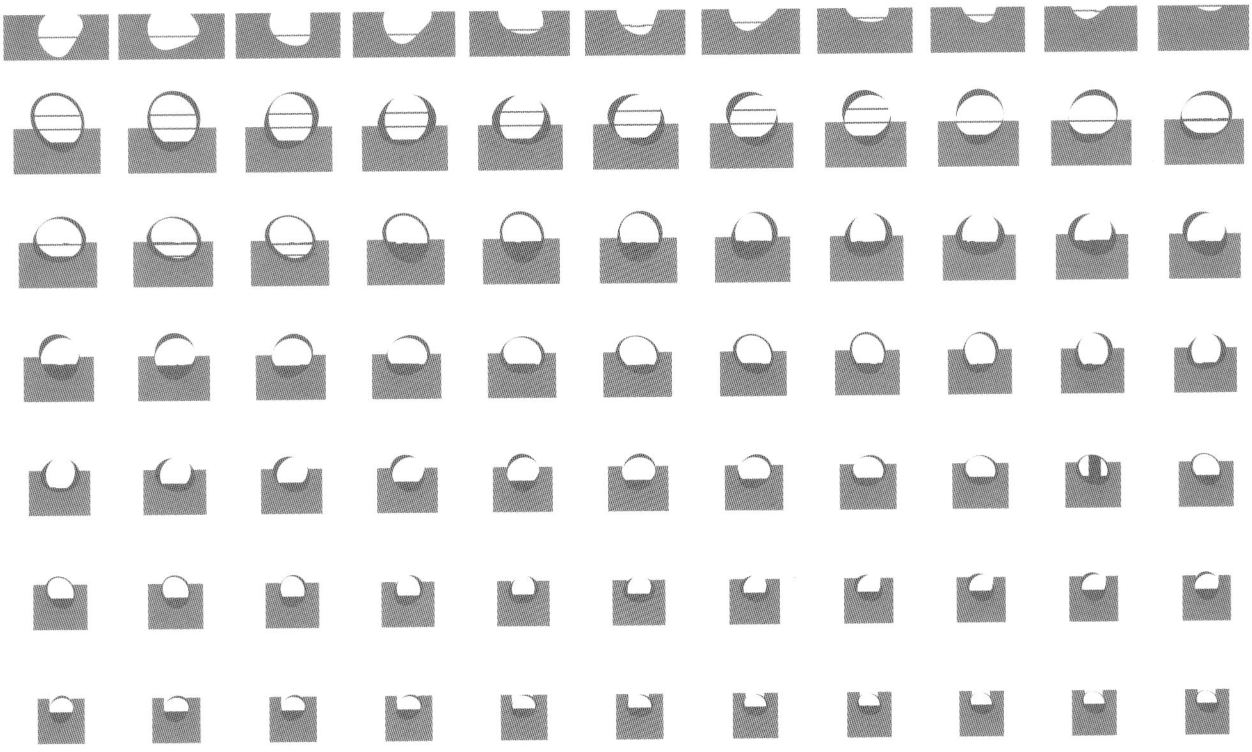

06

01-04 | Mayra Mahmood
05, 06 | Berk Eraslan

01

02

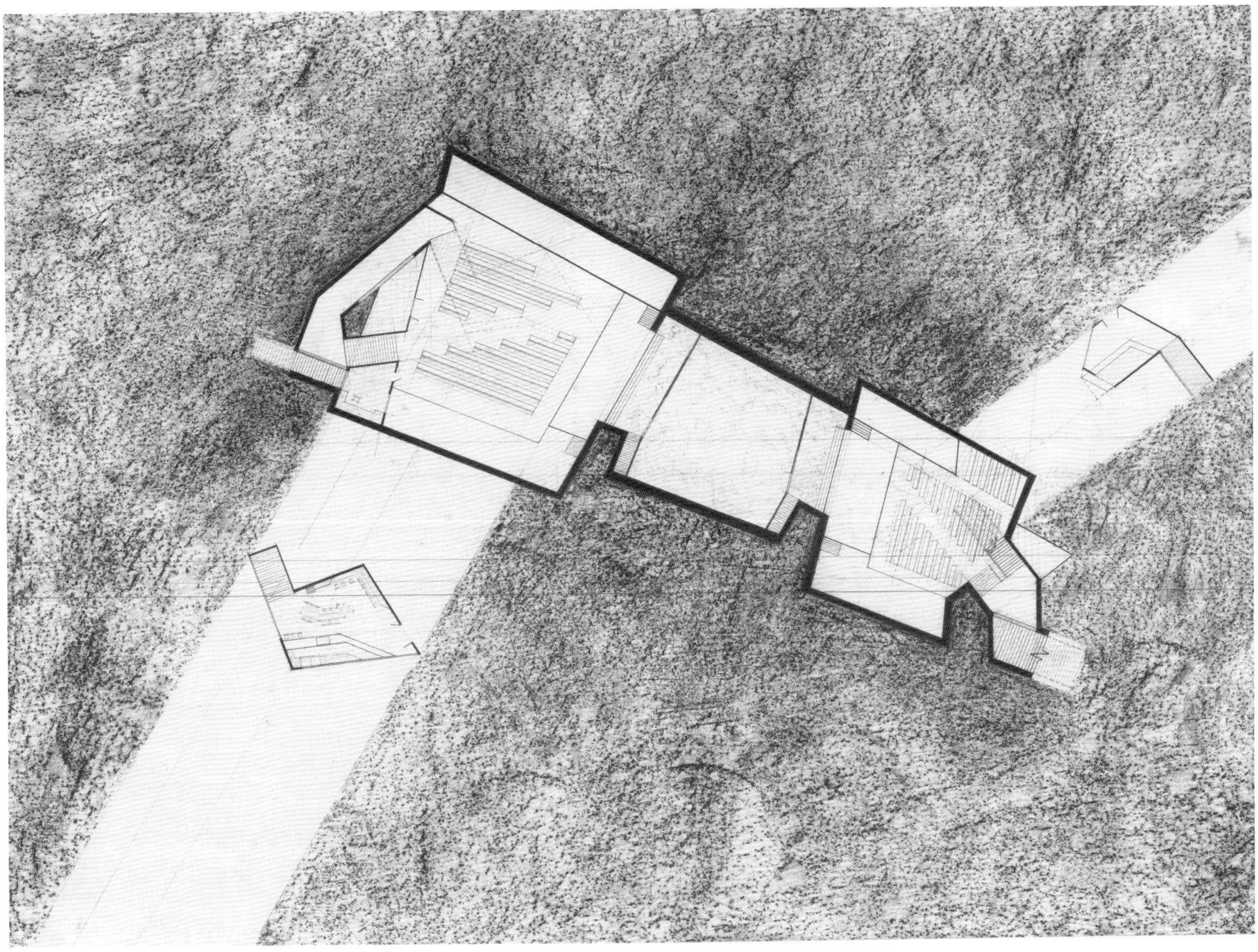

03

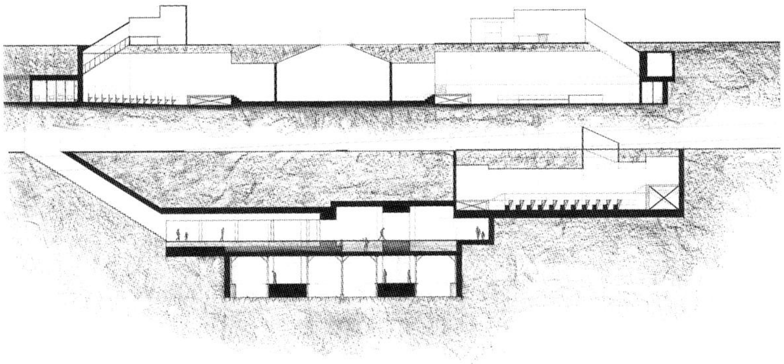

04

01, 03, 04 | Christin Hu
02 | Daniel Restrepo

4th SEMESTER DESIGN

FACULTY
Nandini Bagchee / Antonio Di Oronzo / Arthur Haritos / Ali Hocek

This studio took on the project of designing a place for children, an elementary school in New York City. The work produced by the four studios proposed critical responses to the question of education and dealt with the contingencies of an urban site and the natural environment. Leading into this project the students interrogated the nature of 'play' by which children come to terms with their social environment and develop cognitive skills. They experimented with the geometry of stereo-metric volumes (Froebel's blocks) and developed a set of rules to construct repeating modules that could be aggregated into a play pavilion. This system was further developed into a classroom and school. In tandem, they analyzed models of early education and precedents of school design from Duiker's Open Air School in Amsterdam (1930) to more recent, innovative, community-built schools such as the METI Handmade School in Bangladesh (2006). This understanding of different models and innovative construction criteria was positioned into the density of lower Manhattan as students proposed their own model for an elementary school in a corner lot on the roof of an existing one story building. The project advanced the student's architectural skills significantly and also made them think critically about the institutions of education in the contemporary city.

Nandini Bagchee
Second Year Design Coordinator

Andy Liu
NANDINI BAGCHEE, CRITIC

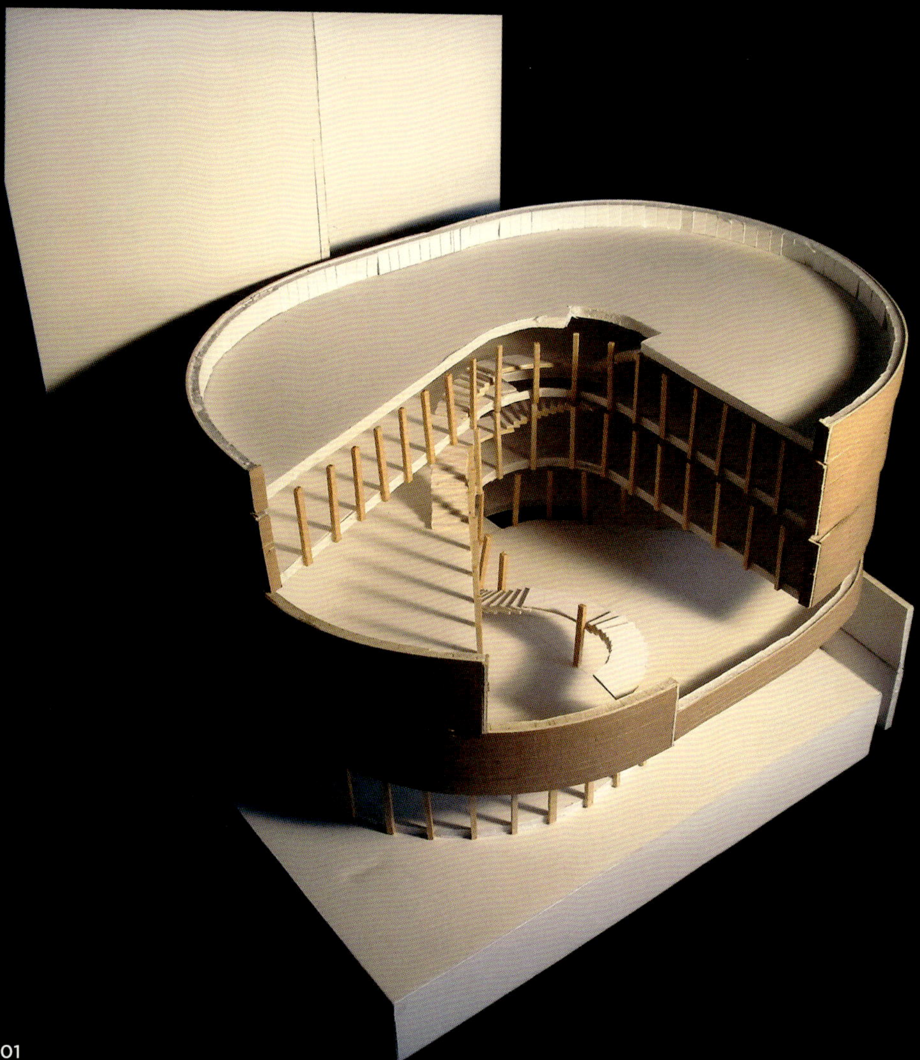

01

02

03

04

01 | Midori Tanabe
02, 03 | Anna Kwiatkowska
04 | Andy Liu

01

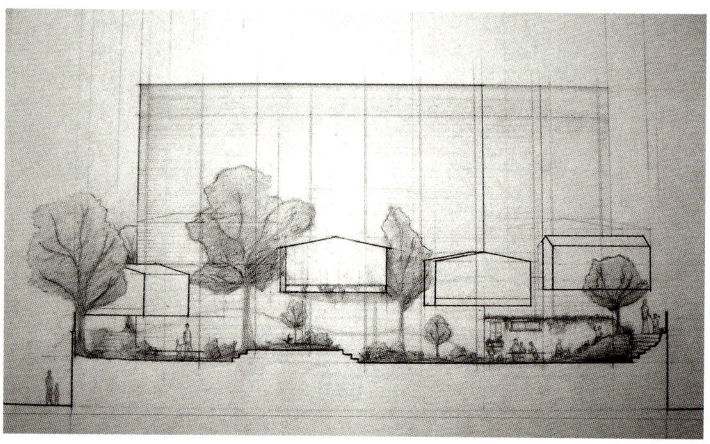

02

03

04

01-03 | Christin Hu
04 | Alanna Lauter

01

02

03

04

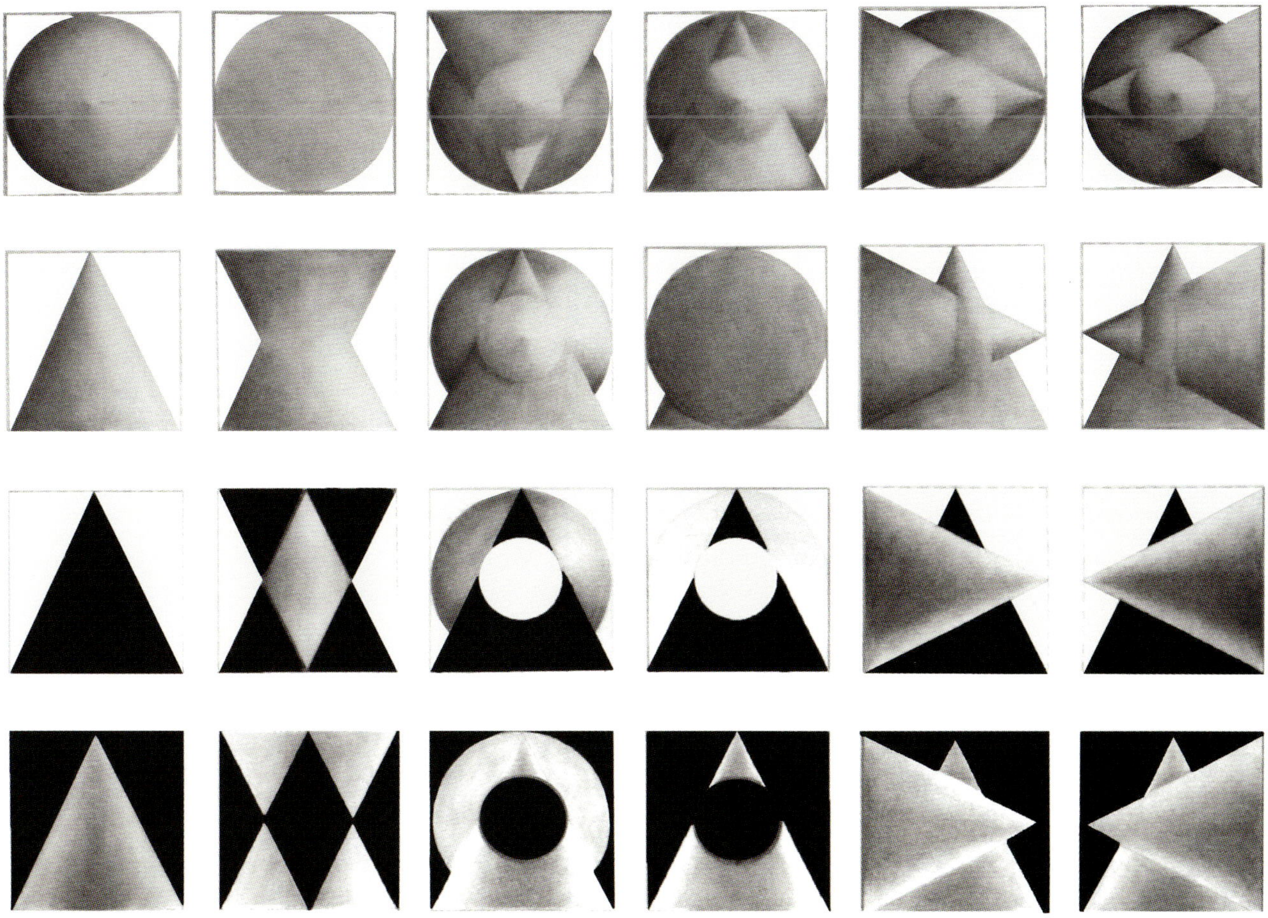

05

01-03 | Berk Eraslan
04, 05 | Stephanie Salazar

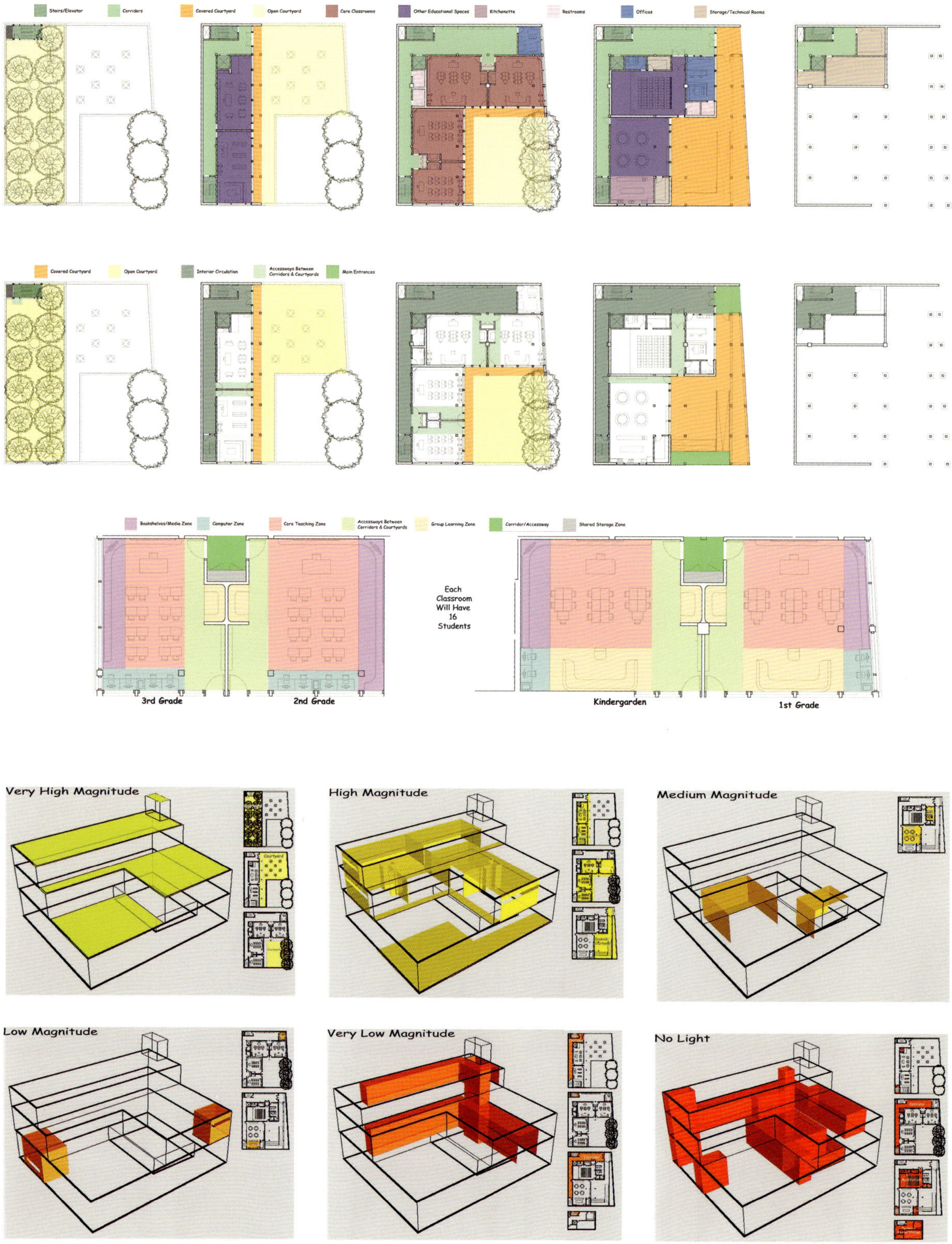
Stairs/Elevator
Corridors
Covered Courtyard
Open Courtyard
Core Classrooms
Other Educational Spaces
Kitchenette
Restrooms
Offices
Storage/Technical Rooms
Covered Courtyard
Open Courtyard
Interior Circulation
Accessways Between Corridors & Courtyards
Main Entrances
Bookshelves/Media Zone
Computer Zone
Core Teaching Zone
Accessways Between Corridors & Courtyards
Group Learning Zone
Corridor/Accessway
Shared Storage Zone
Each Classroom Will Have 16 Students
3rd Grade
2nd Grade
Kindergarden
1st Grade
Very High Magnitude
High Magnitude
Medium Magnitude
Low Magnitude
Very Low Magnitude
No Light

01

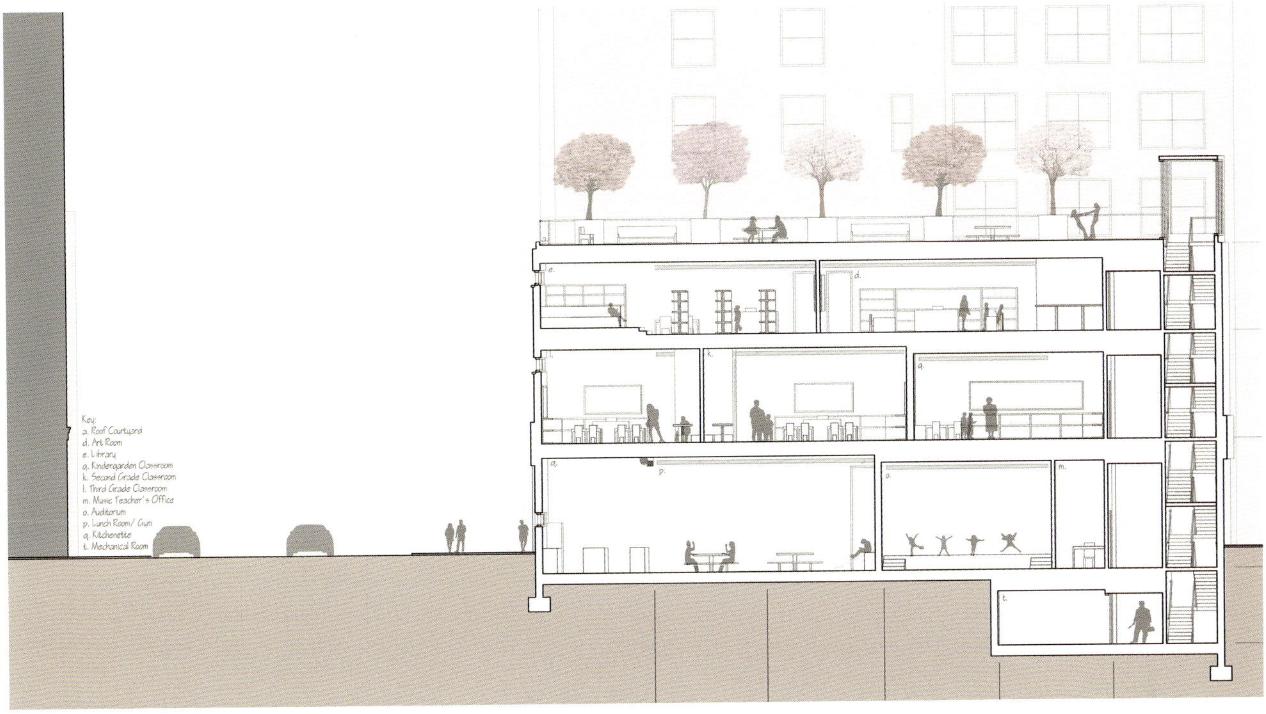

02

03

01, 02 | Katherine Serrano Sosa
03 | Lenny Chen

5th SEMESTER DESIGN

FACULTY
Alberto Foyo / Ivan Rosa /
Elisabetta Terragni / Christian Volkmann

The semester focused on the importance of "site specificity" and its relationship with the process of design. This required close attention to patterns of living, the nature of the site, issues of materiality, and the way of joining the components of a building.

The choices made in designing and specifying building components needed to respond to both practical requirements and the conceptual integrity of the project, were also examined. Furthermore, the project needed to achieve a scale of its own, and a proportionality, or appropriateness, for our way of living, for the body and its habitat. Students worked on two connected exercises in the course of the semester. Exercise 1: Body movement/tools/relations in everyday living. Starting from body movements and objects of daily use [from clothing to electronic equipment, from private spaces to collective interaction], we created a database of situations by which students could familiarize themselves with the size, proportion, and nature of habitable spaces. Exercise 2: Design process: "Two Residential Units" with a gathering space in Bushwick, Brooklyn. A nest for dreaming, a shelter for imagining. Our project tried to discover how human habitation translates into space, and how space affects its inhabitants. All houses recall other houses, and many houses serve as sites of memory for their inhabitants. As we move in the course of a lifetime from one house to another, we tend to recreate sites of memory as well as acquire new spaces. We explored the possibility of integrating all spaces (without simply segregating some, such as corridors or bathrooms as having purely functional purposes) in such a way that the house becomes a small universe of its own. Students mapped out the spaces with an eye to site and with regard to the family story they've invented for the project.

Elisabetta Terragni
Third Year Design Coordinator

Demir Purisic
ELISABETTA TERRAGNI, CRITIC

01

02

03

04

01-04 | Christian Camacho / Diana Zwetzich / Nooreen Kagzi / Tiffany Urosa / Billy McMillen / Evan Kalogiannis / Moe Myat Thu / Marcus Tung / Magdalena Checo / Deswacy Powell / Melissa Santana / Veronica Rivas

01

02

03

04

05

06

07

01, 02 | Sewina Lee
03-05 | Jacline Vargas
06, 07 | Sayra Yepez

01

02

03

04

05

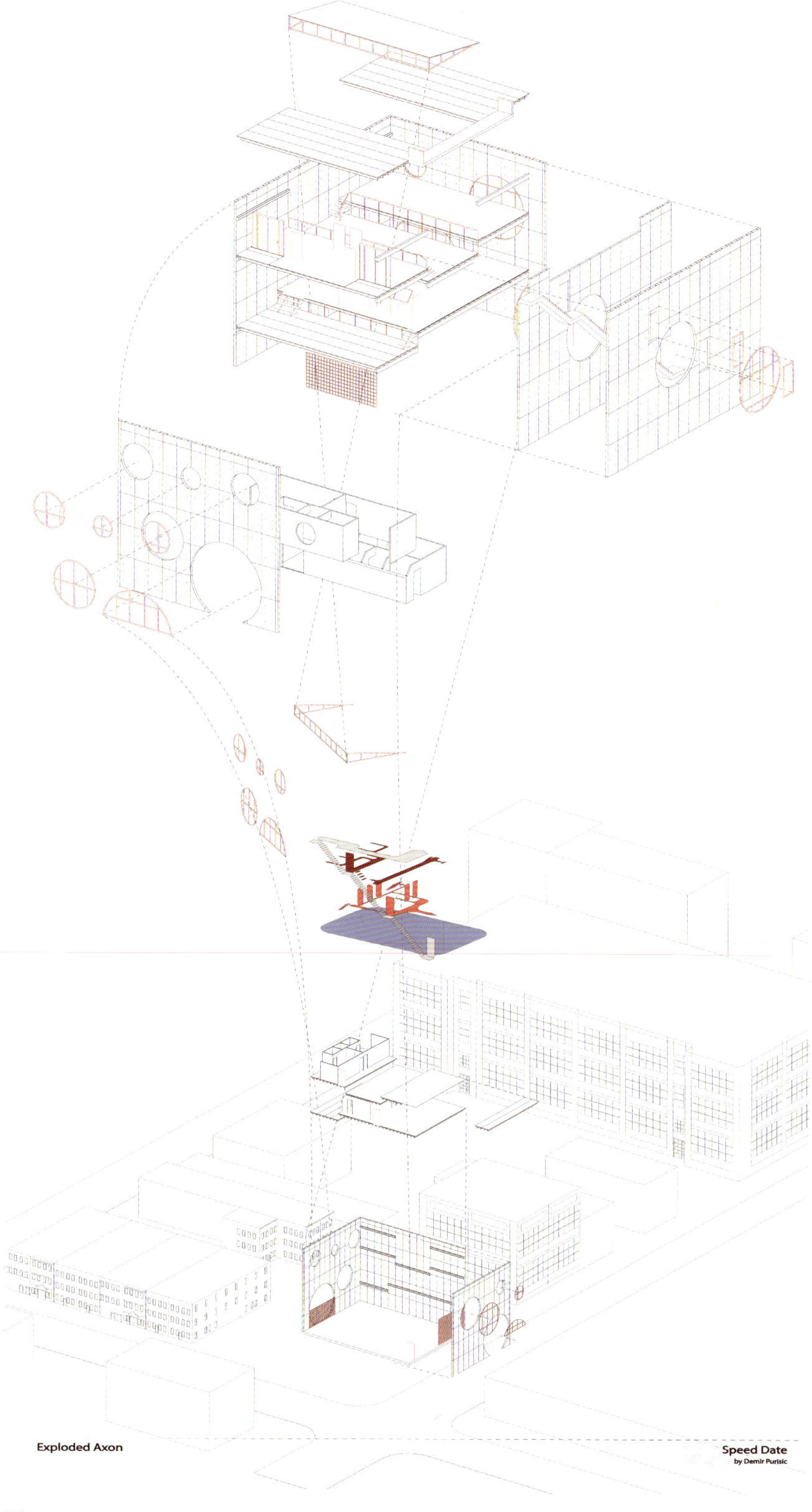

06

01, 02 | Muhammad Saleh
03-05 | Jeffrey Bermudez
06 | Demir Purisic

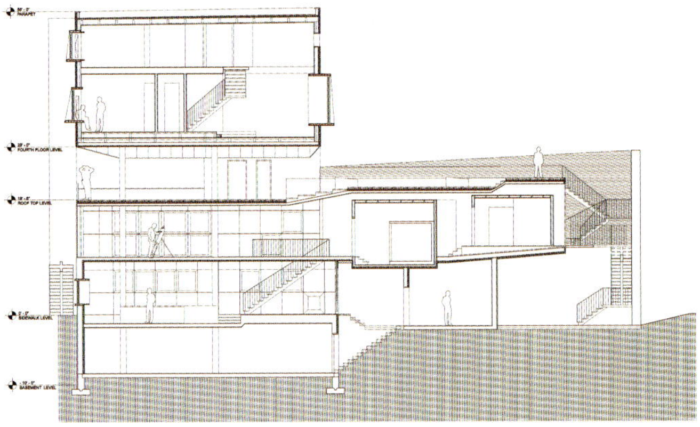

01

02

03

04

05

01-03 | Ermira Kasapi
04 | Ryan Hung
05 | Mary Rizaldo

6th SEMESTER DESIGN

FACULTY
Alberto Foyo / Adam Hayes /
Fabian Llonch / Ivan Rosa

The studio developed a concept for the The Harlem School of the Arts combining a number of public agencies with great missions, Yvette L. Campbell, President and CEO of HSA and Tony Griffin, Director of the J. Max Bond Center on Design for the Just City were our demanding and visionary client and mentors in transforming the existing building and adjacent areas in an even more efficient, inspiring structure open to the Community.

The principal purpose was to embrace the citizenry's concerns for their children and their environment in connection with their immediate surroundings. The Harlem School of the Arts (HSA) stands apart among the premier arts institutions in New York City as the sole provider of quality arts education in 4 disciplines - music, dance, theater and visual arts - in an award-winning 37,000 square foot facility nestled at the base of Harlem's historic Hamilton Heights. The conjunction of a resident population, transportation, and pressing environmental issues, make for an opportune site where educational purposes meet practical necessities.

A public building inevitably connects individuals with the society at large, linking the private with the public, the singular with the collective. It establishes a location for the negotiation of these relationships. Beyond these central concerns, the semester's work gave importance to "site specificity", re-using and transforming and its relationship with the process of design. This required close attention to urban patterns, code and regulation, materiality and respect and interest in memory and history. Furthermore, the project aimed to achieve a scale of its own and a proportionality, or appropriateness, for our way of experiencing the city.

Elisabetta Terragni
Third Year Design Coordinator

Christian Camacho / Alvaro Almada
FABIAN LLONCH, CRITIC

01

02

03

01-03 | Muhammad Saleh / Cesar Mesias
Nicholas Siriban / Sayra Yepez

01

02

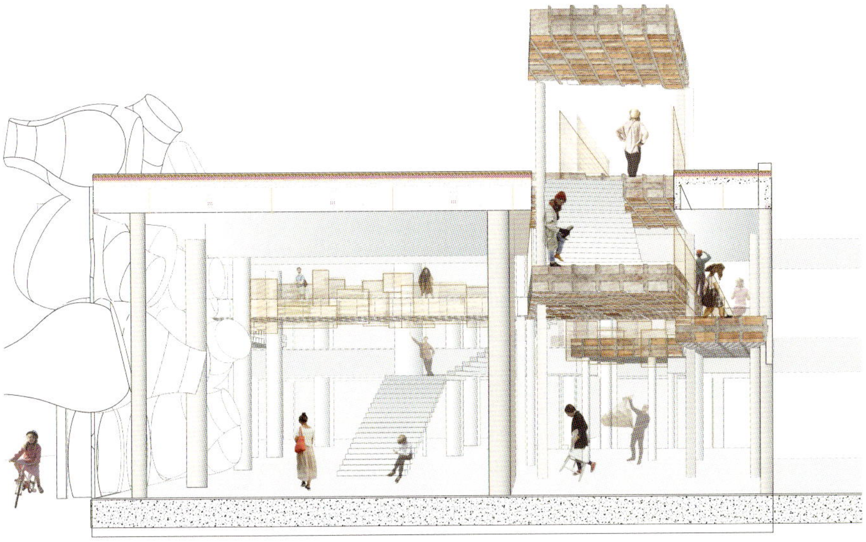

03

04

01, 02 | Demir Purisic / Jose Jimenez / Diana Zwetzich / Ermira Kasapi
03, 04 | Melissa Santana / Madelyn Pena / Simit Christian

01

02

03

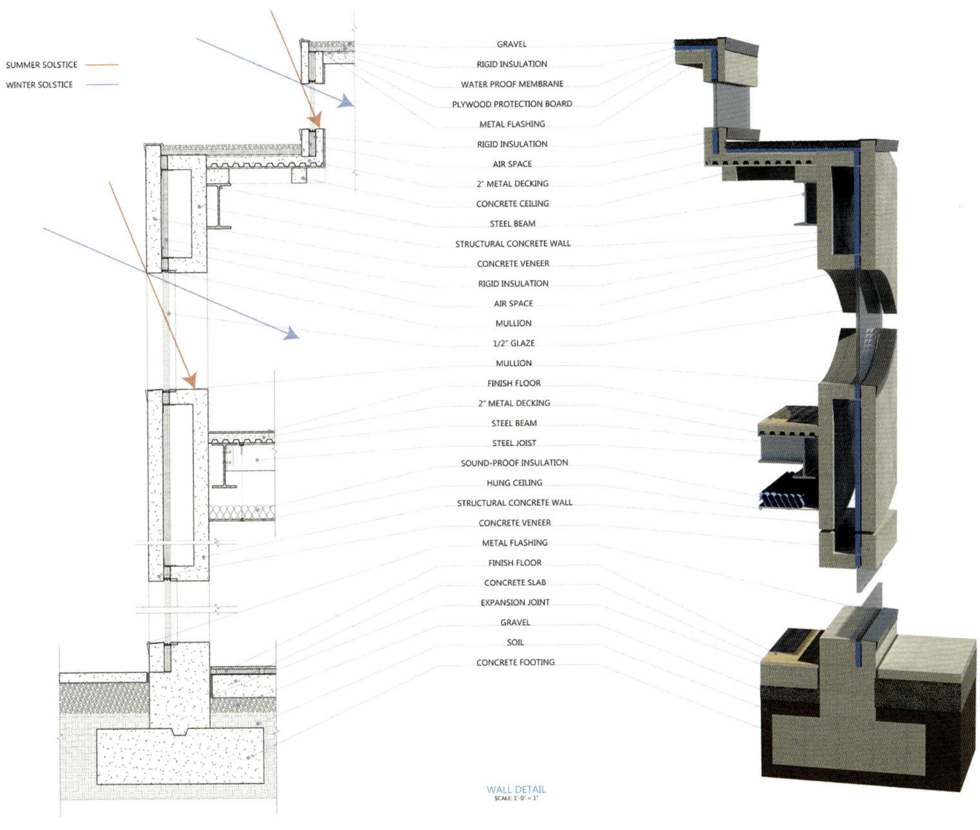

04

01, 02 | Christian Camacho / Alvaro Almada
03, 04 | Magdalena Checo / Marcus Tung

01

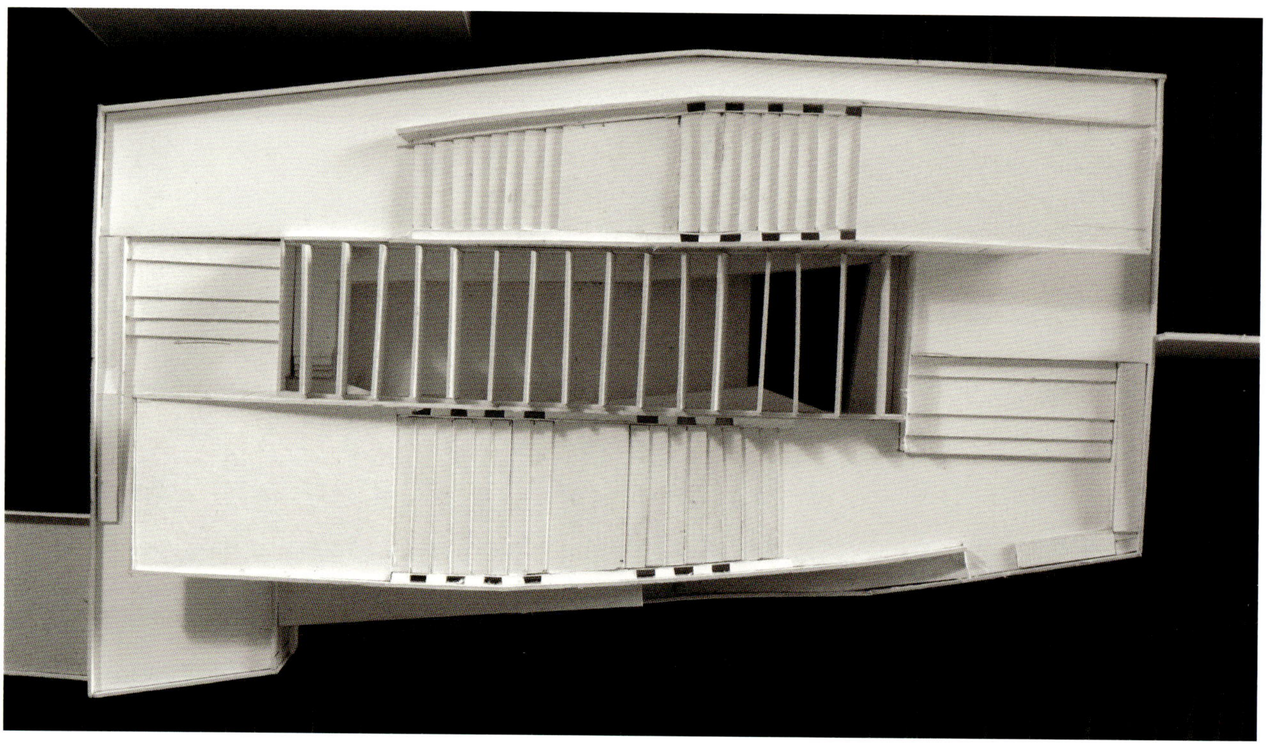

02

03

04

05

01, 02 | Jacline Vargas / Ryan Hung
03-05 | Sewina Lee / Tiffany Urosa

7th SEMESTER DESIGN

FACULTY
Timothy Matthew Collins / Peter Gisolfi / Joan Krevlin / Julio Salcedo-Fernandez / June Williamson

This studio investigates the design of sustainable multi-unit housing in an urban context and is organized in a series of phases that include: typological research, site analysis, program analysis, concept generation, and design development. The initial exercise is an investigation of manipulating unit and housing types. This is followed by a rigorous context analysis leading to an urban design proposition for adding housing to enhance the campus setting and its ecological performance. Once the building siting is established, students proceed with analysis of program and further precedent studies, incorporating alternate housing philosophies. The building design process is organized around studies of massing and circulation, unit and suite layouts, open space, façade, and building details and technologies.

Strategies for sustainable design are explored through context and site analysis, as well as in precedent studies. A short design assignment emphasizes energy conserving design strategies to incorporate into building and urban solutions.

In the fall of 2012, students sited and designed an on-campus Residence Hall for approximately 100 students, as well as six small faculty apartments. Each studio investigated a different higher-education campus: 1) Lehman College/CUNY (Collins), 2) College of Mount St. Vincent (Krevlin), 3) Bryn Mawr College (Salcedo), and 4) Hofstra University (Williamson).

June Williamson
Fourth Year Design Coordinator

Chrisoula Kapelonis
TIMOTHY MATHEW COLLINS, CRITIC

01

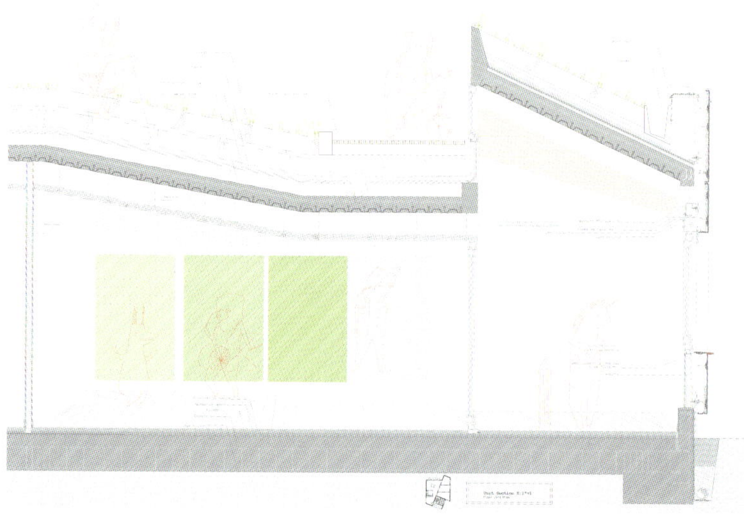

02

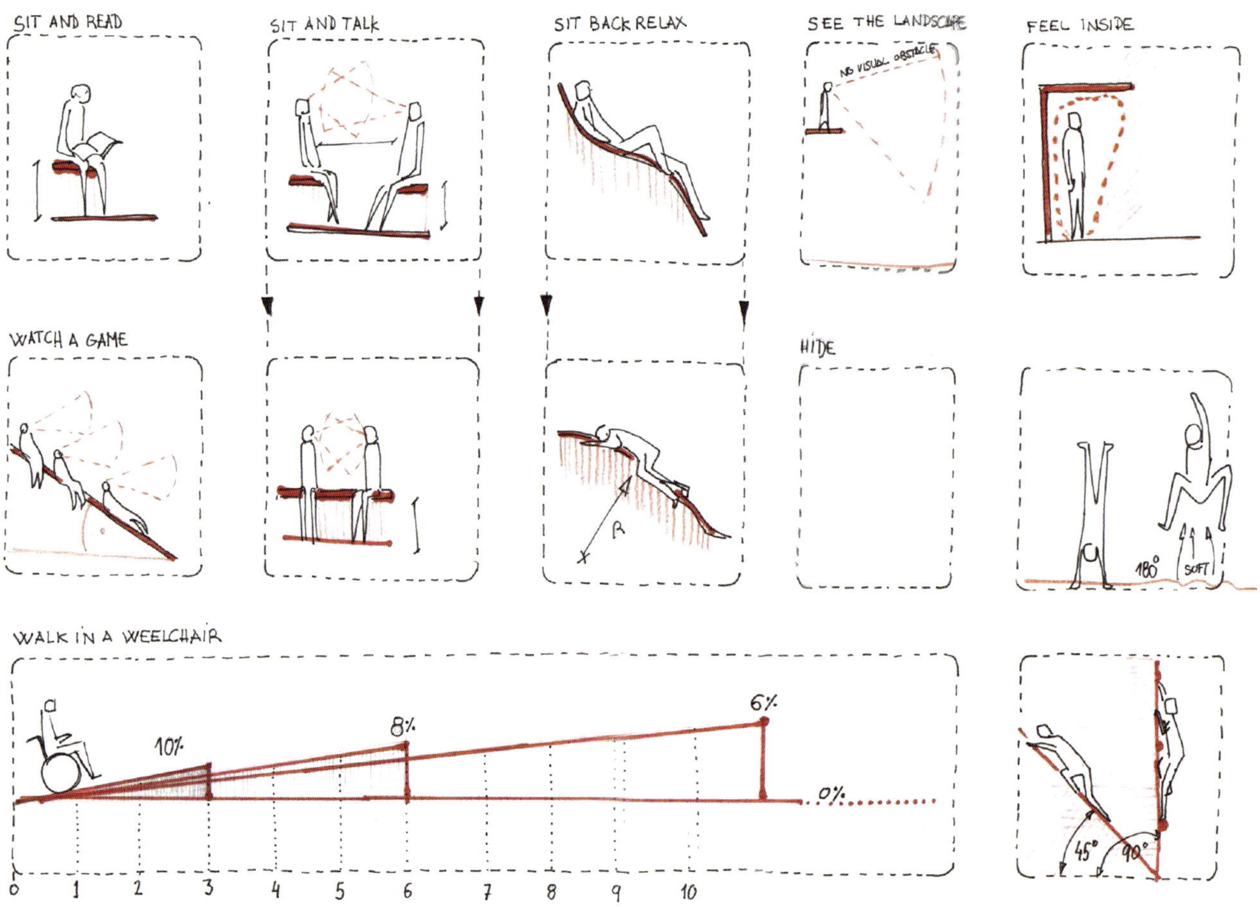
SIT AND READ
SIT AND TALK
SIT BACK RELAX
SEE THE LANDSCAPE
NO VISUAL OBSTACLE
FEEL INSIDE
WATCH A GAME
R
HIDE
180°
SOFT
WALK IN A WEELCHAIR
10%
8%
6%
0%
0 1 2 3 4 5 6 7 8 9 10
45°
90°

03

04

01-03 | Clara Dios Diez
04 | Chrisoula Kapelonis

01

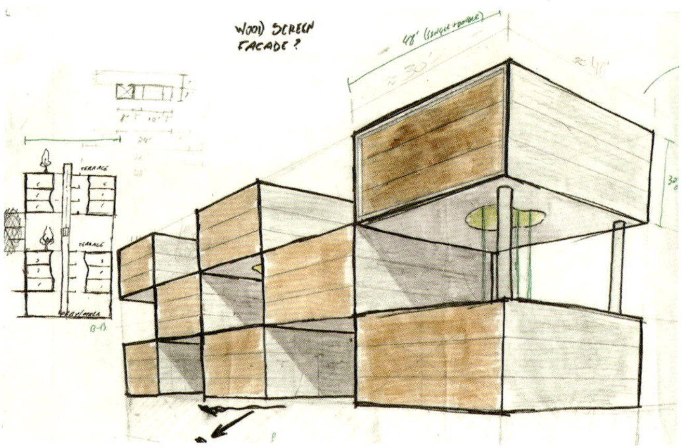

02

03

04

01, 02 | Anthony Girón
03 | Carolina Olszewska
04 | Idan Saragosti

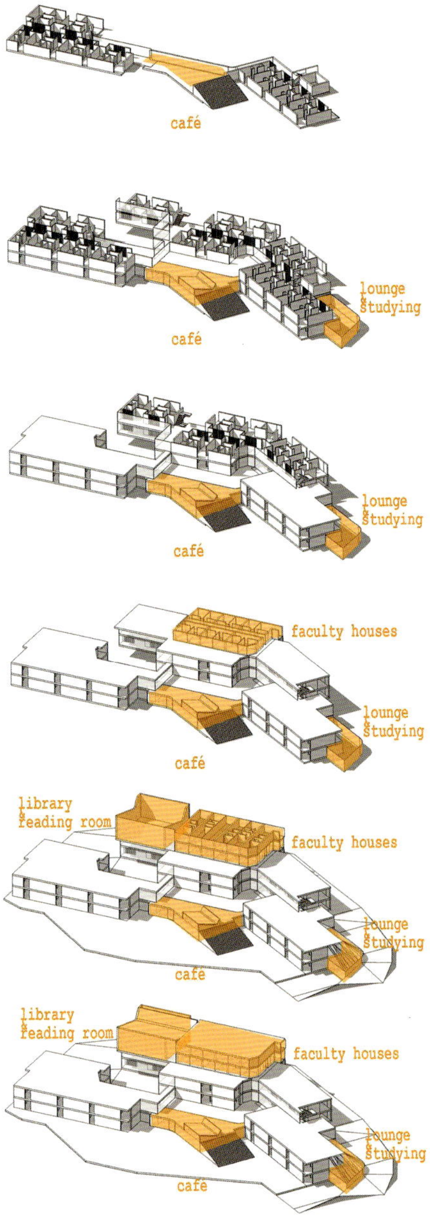
café
lounge & studying
faculty houses
library & reading room

01

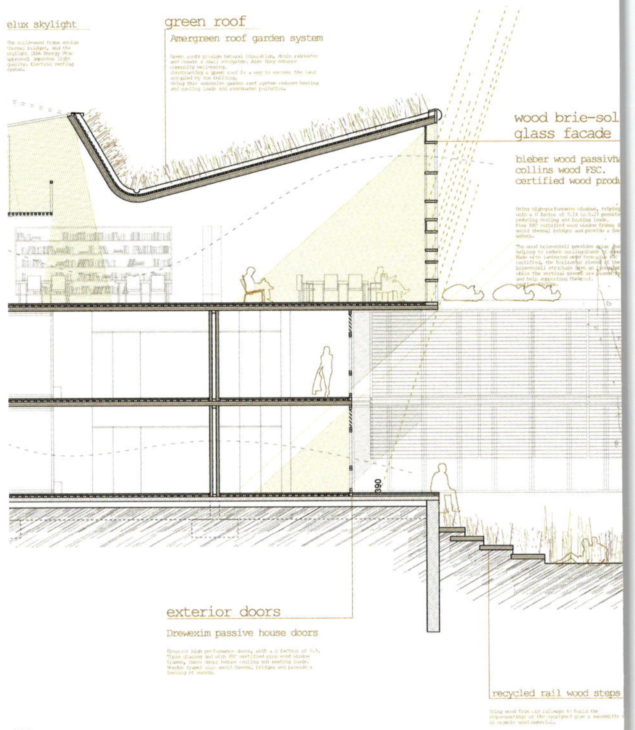
elux skylight
green roof
Amergreen roof garden system
wood brie-sol
glass facade
bieber wood passivn
collins wood FSC.
certified wood produ
exterior doors
Drewexim passive house doors
recycled rail wood steps

02

03

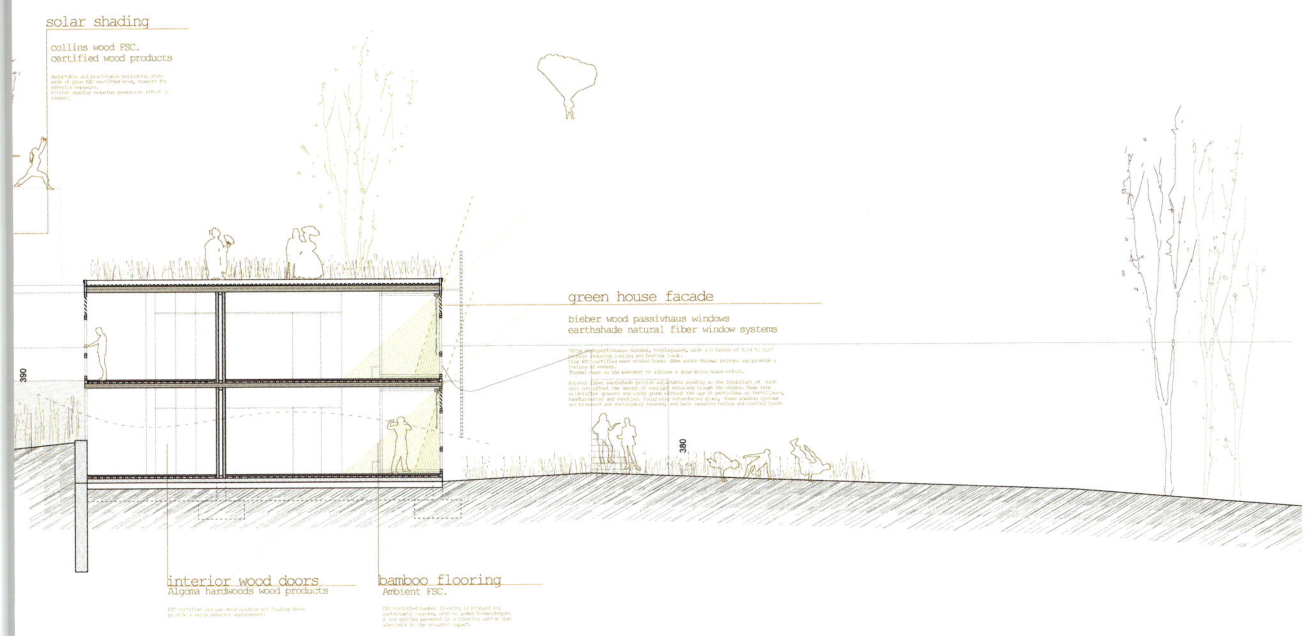

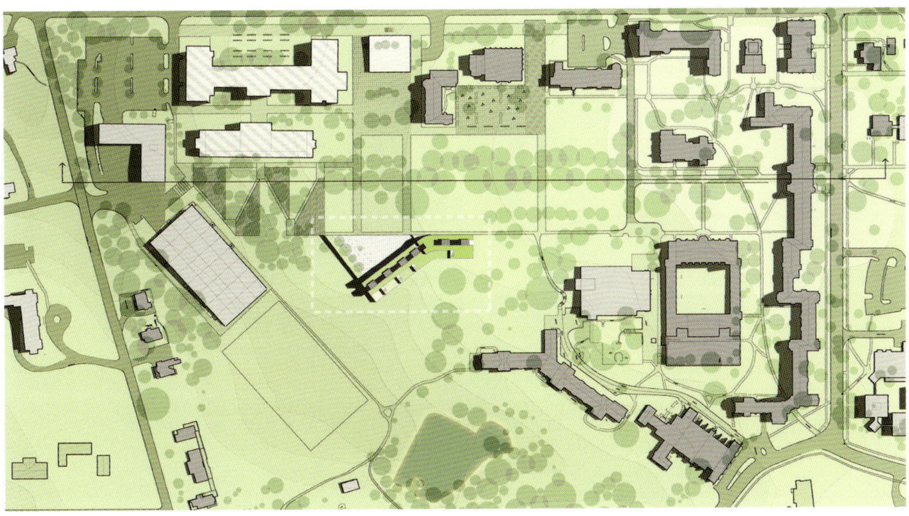

04

01, 02 | Berta Cuso Cuquerella
03, 04 | Tatum Tan-Tiongco

01

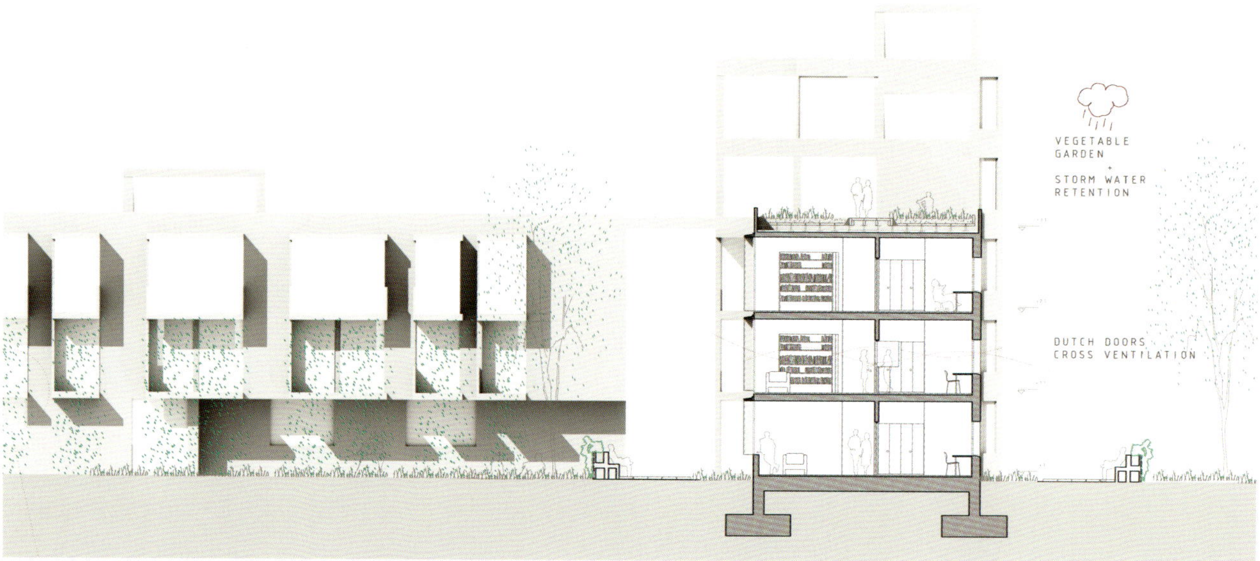
VEGETABLE GARDEN
+
STORM WATER RETENTION
DUTCH DOORS
CROSS VENTILATION

02

03

04

05

01, 02 | Gemma Diaz Tortajada
03-05 | Chris Innelli

8th SEMESTER DESIGN

FACULTY
Timothy Matthew Collins / Joan Krevlin / Martin Stigsgaard / June Williamson

This semester focuses on public buildings of medium size (30-70,000 sq ft) and on the application of learning in structural and construction systems. The building types studied range from places of assembly to cultural and educational facilities. The semester began with an intense charrette for an international competition, followed by an in-depth precedent analysis of structural systems as applied in an exemplary building. Students then proceeded with site and context analysis, program analysis, conceptual design, and design development with a particular emphasis on innovative structural systems design, performative building skins, and open/public space design and sequencing (including means of egress and ADA compliance).

In the spring of 2013, the studio formed a relationship in Brooklyn with the Atlantic Avenue BID (Building Improvement District) to propose exciting alternative uses for a vacant site on the troubled block between Boerum Place and Smith Street, commonly known as "the gap" on an otherwise vibrant Atlantic Avenue. Each studio proposed a different program for the site: 1) Urban Resource Center (Collins), 2) Culinary Arts College (Krevlin), 3) Atlantic Avenue Sound Lab (Stigsgaard), and 4) Digital Fab Lab and Industrial Crafts Museum (Williamson).

The final projects were exibited in a storefront in Boerum Hill, Brooklyn, and compiled into a booklet that was presented to the BID.

June Williamson
Fourth Year Design Coordinator

Filipp Blyakher
JOAN KREVLIN, CRITIC

01

02

03

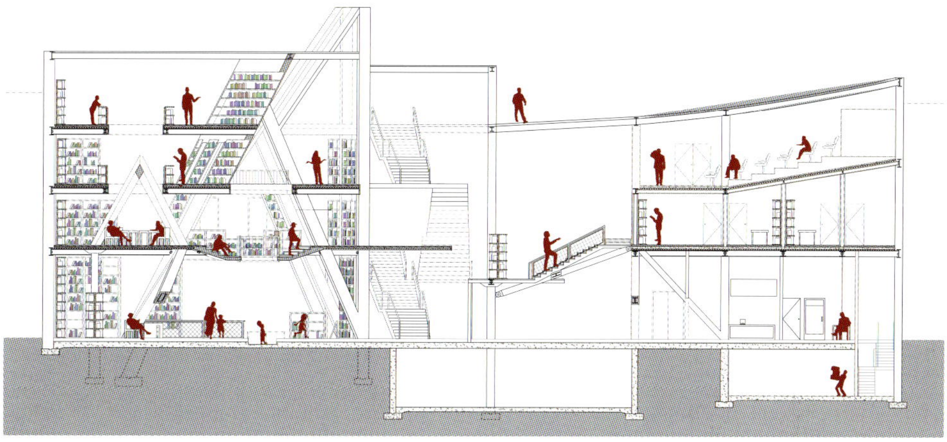

04

01, 02 | Idan Saragosti
03, 04 | Melinda Siew

01

02

03

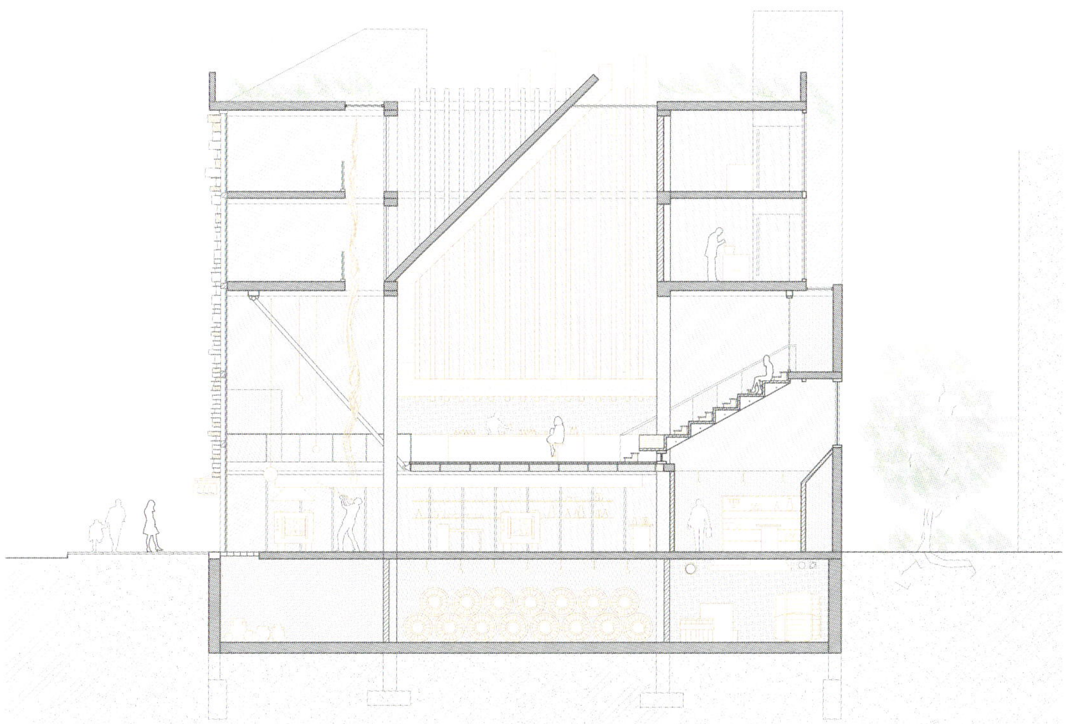

04

01, 02 | Chrisoula Kapelonis
03 | Berta Cuso Cuquerella
04 | Filipp Blyakher

01

02

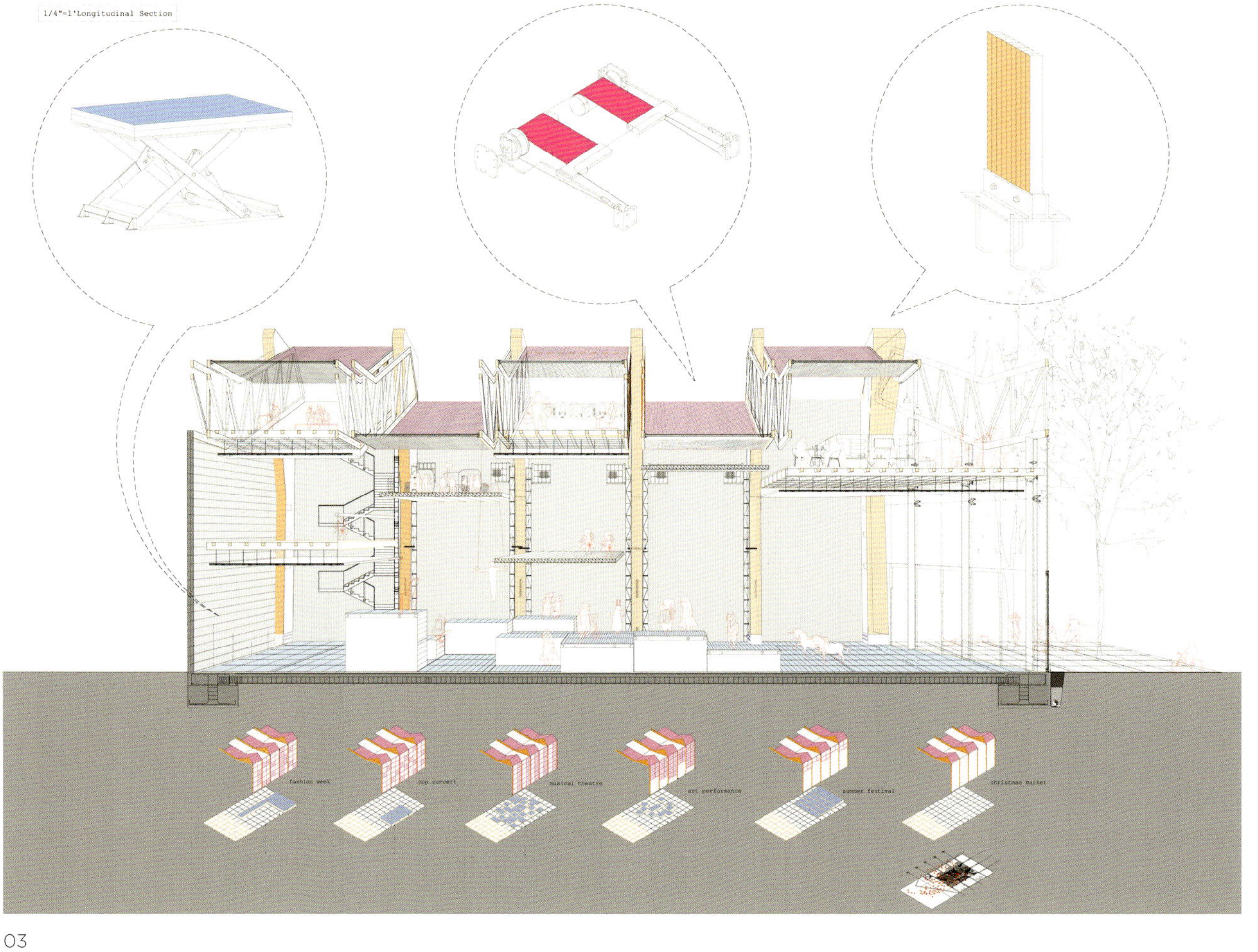
1/4"=1'Longitudinal Section
fashion week
pop concert
musical theatre
art performance
summer festival
christmas market

03

04

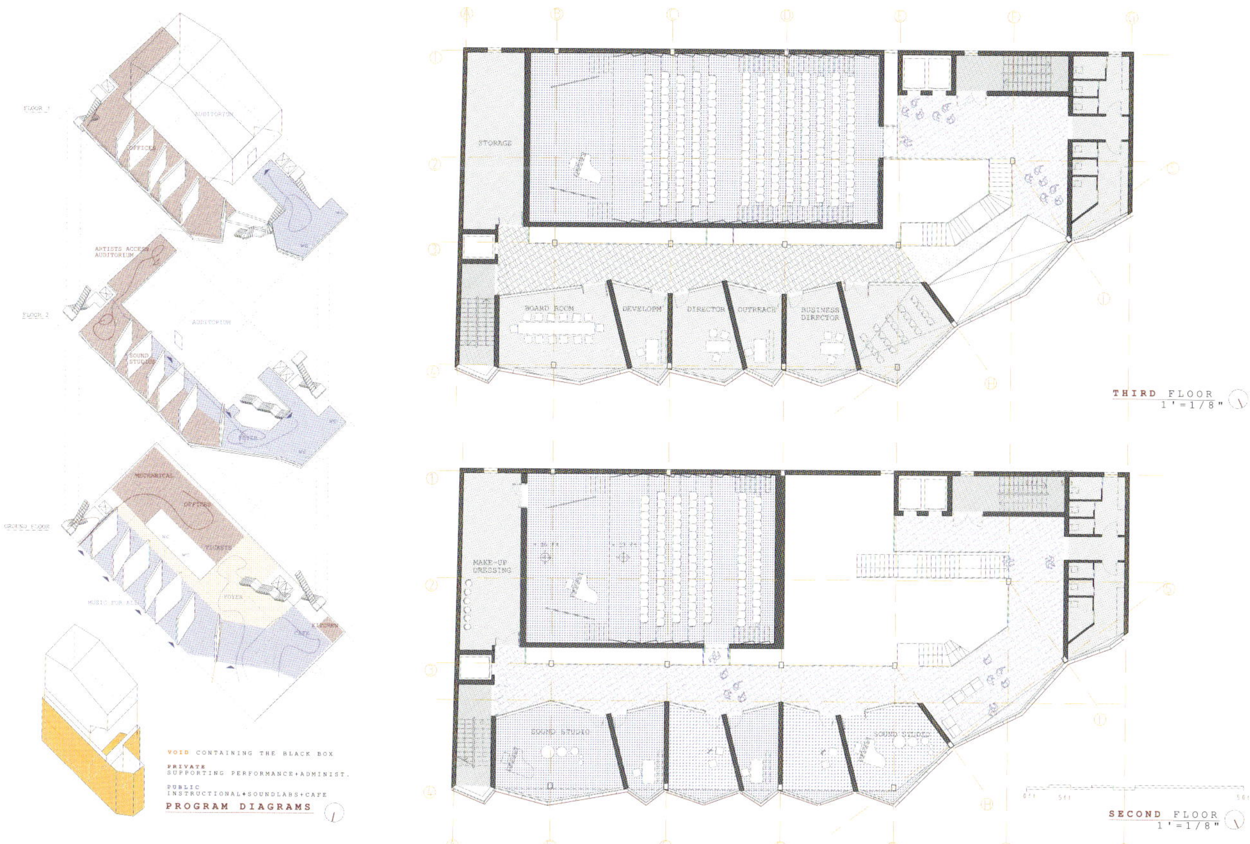

05

01-03 | Clara Dios Diez
04-05 | Gemma Diaz Tortajada

01

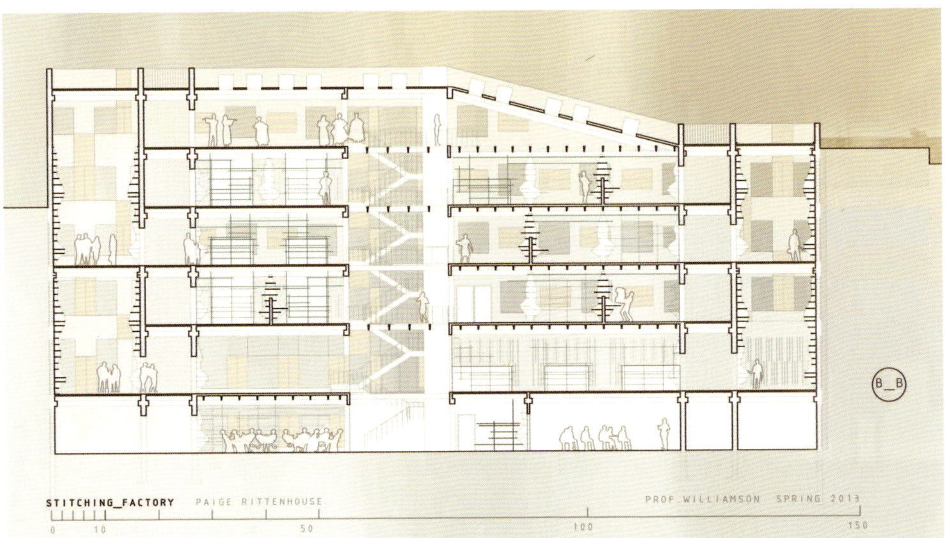
B_B
STITCHING_FACTORY
PAIGE RITTENHOUSE
PROF WILLIAMSON SPRING 2013
0
10
50
100
150

02

03

04

01, 02 | Paige Rittenhouse
03, 04 | Chris Innelli

COMPREHENSIVE DESIGN

FACULTY
Jacob Alspector / Lance Jay Brown / Caleb Crawford / Jeremy Edmiston / Vanessa Keith / Gary McNeil

The SSA/CCNY year-long, two-semester, fifth-year Comprehensive Design Studio provides a unique opportunity for exploration and pursuit of original, individual, and independent architectural research, analyses, and synthesis within the collaborative, critical and interactive studio framework including peers, professors, consultants, and guest critics. The year is structured to integrate, comprehensively, all previous architectural teachings and display an expertise appropriate to an advanced undergraduate seeking a professional degree. The synthesis of original thought, individual exploration, collaborative criticism and integration of knowledge and learning should ideally lead to synergistic revelation and transcendence of mere architectural problem solving.

Each student's project is framed to explore a specific idea. In the first semester of Comprehensive Design the selected architectural program, context, site, appropriate technology, and zoning are analyzed, appropriate case studies are researched and alternative concepts and schematic designs are developed. Students are challenged to fully engage evolving social, technical, and aesthetic aspects of their project. A complete array of drawings and models of a selected schematic design are presented for review at semester's end. The second semester allows for revisions based on criticism from the mid year review, detailed investigation of structure, skin, and climate control, and detail design development of the entirety including the supportive and integrated exterior and interior landscapes, furnishings, lighting, and materials. Towards the end of the second semester students concentrate on finalizing project documentation and communication in readiness for the final Comprehensive Design Studio review.

Lance Jay Brown, FAIA
Comprehensive Design Coordinator

Artur Dabrowski
JEREMY EDMISTON, CRITIC

GENERAL FIRST FLOOR PLAN | SCALE 1/16" = 1'-0"

"A Building should appear to grow easily from its site and be shaped to harmonize with its surroundings if Nature is manifest there."
_Frank Lloyd Wright

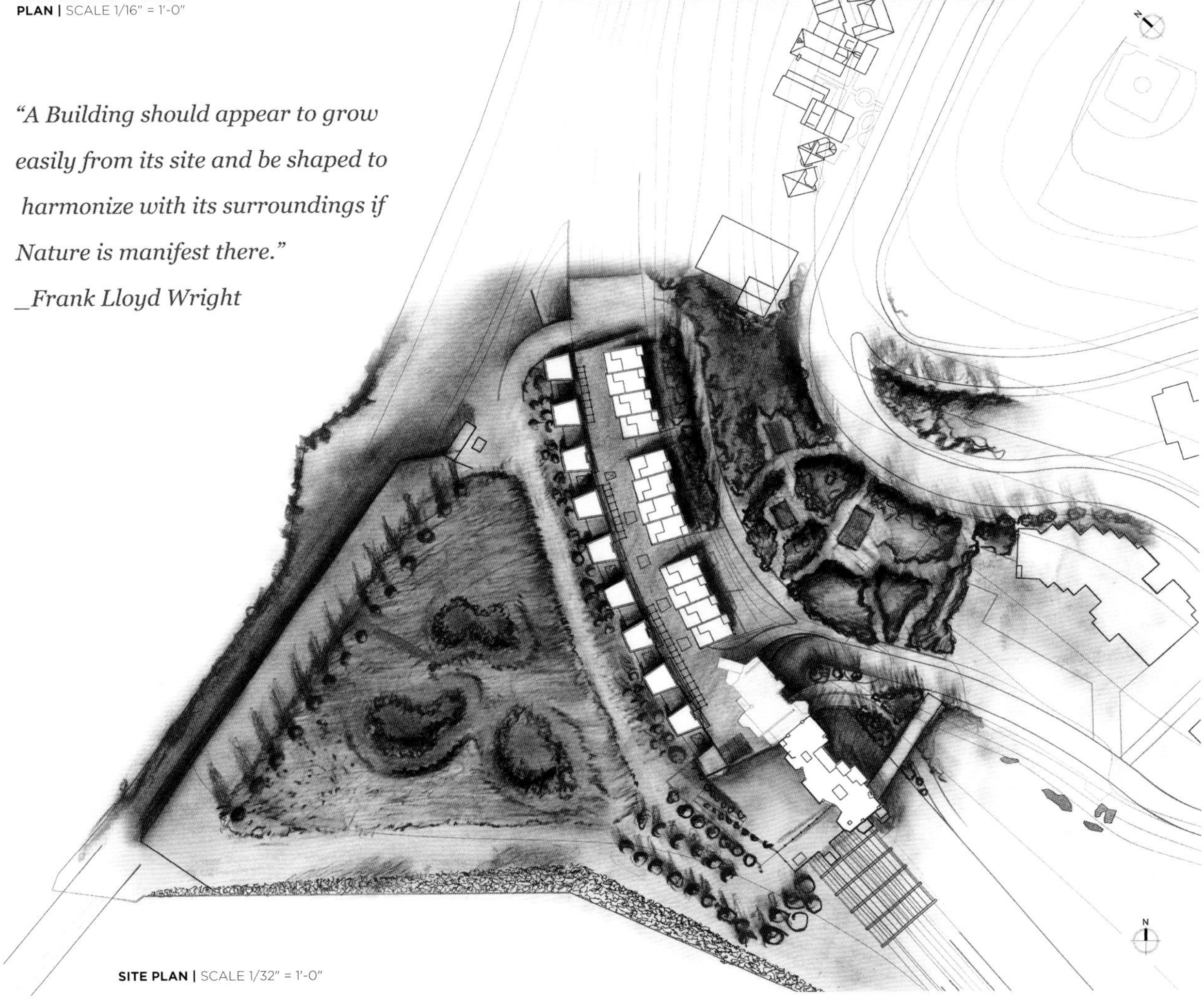

SITE PLAN | SCALE 1/32" = 1'-0"

01

02

03

04

01-04 | Tate Sumner

01

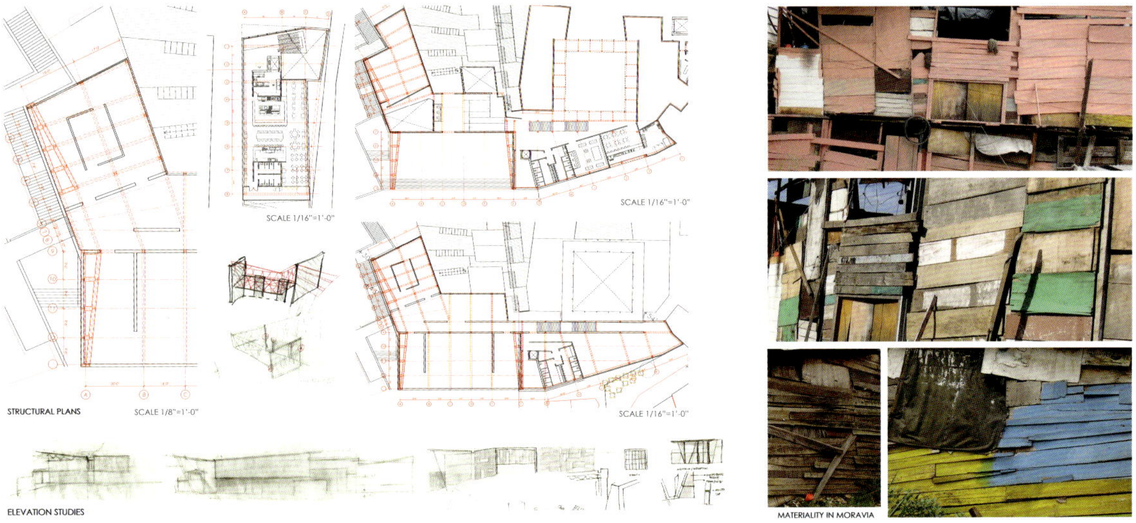
SCALE 1/16"=1'-0"
SCALE 1/16"=1'-0"
STRUCTURAL PLANS
SCALE 1/8"=1'-0"
SCALE 1/16"=1'-0"
ELEVATION STUDIES
MATERIALITY IN MORAVIA

02

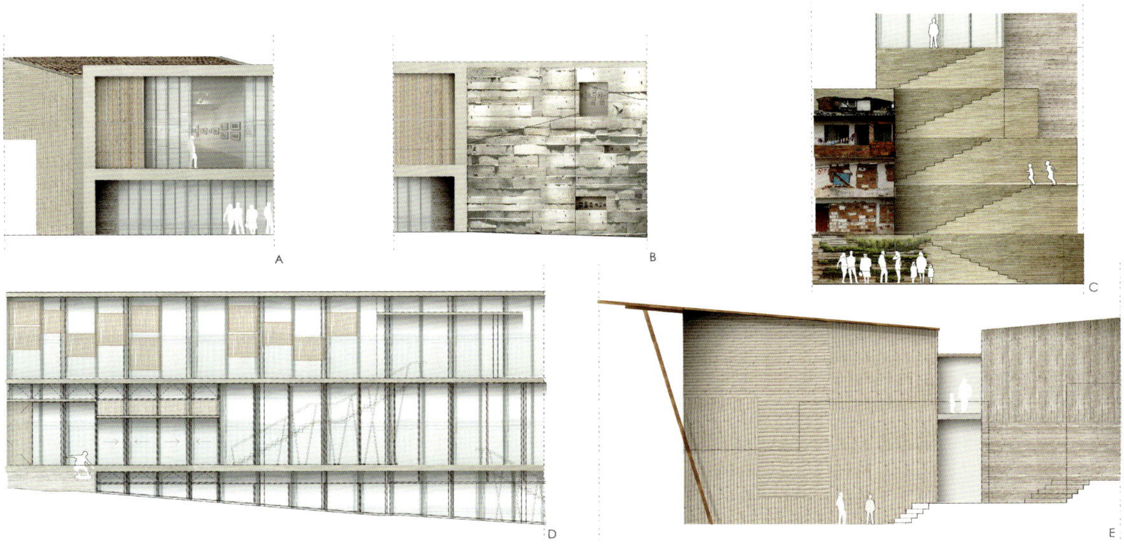
A
B
C
D
E

03

MUSEUM AS A PLACE OF APPROPIATION OF MEMORIES

The museum appropiates the negative spaces left by the traces of the past. It anchors itself between the main circulation of the park and the neighboring residential context. It meanders in an attempt to respond to the houses that frame it. *Remember* becomes the core of the programs both in plan and section. It's adjacency to the ruins of a few houses delineates the area where educate and remember meet.

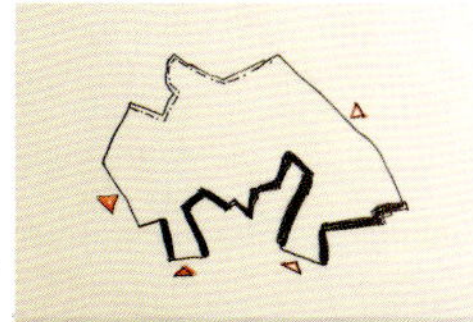

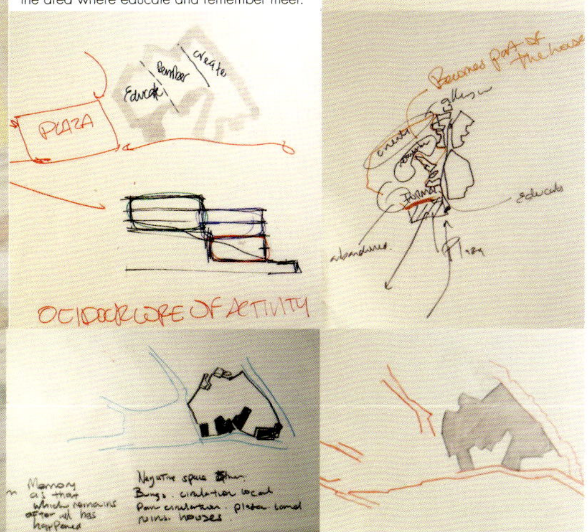

04

01-04 | Veronica Velasquez

Level 15
146' - 0"
Level 14
136' - 0"
Level 13
126' - 0"
Level 12
116' - 0"
Level 11
106' - 0"
Level 10
96' - 0"
Level 9
86' - 0"
Level 8
76' - 0"
Level 7
66' - 0"
Level 6
56' - 0"
Level 5
46' - 0"
Level 4
36' - 0"
Level 3
26' - 0"
Level 2
12' - 0"
Level 1
0' - 0"
0
15
45'

01

1
2
3
4
5
6
7
8

02

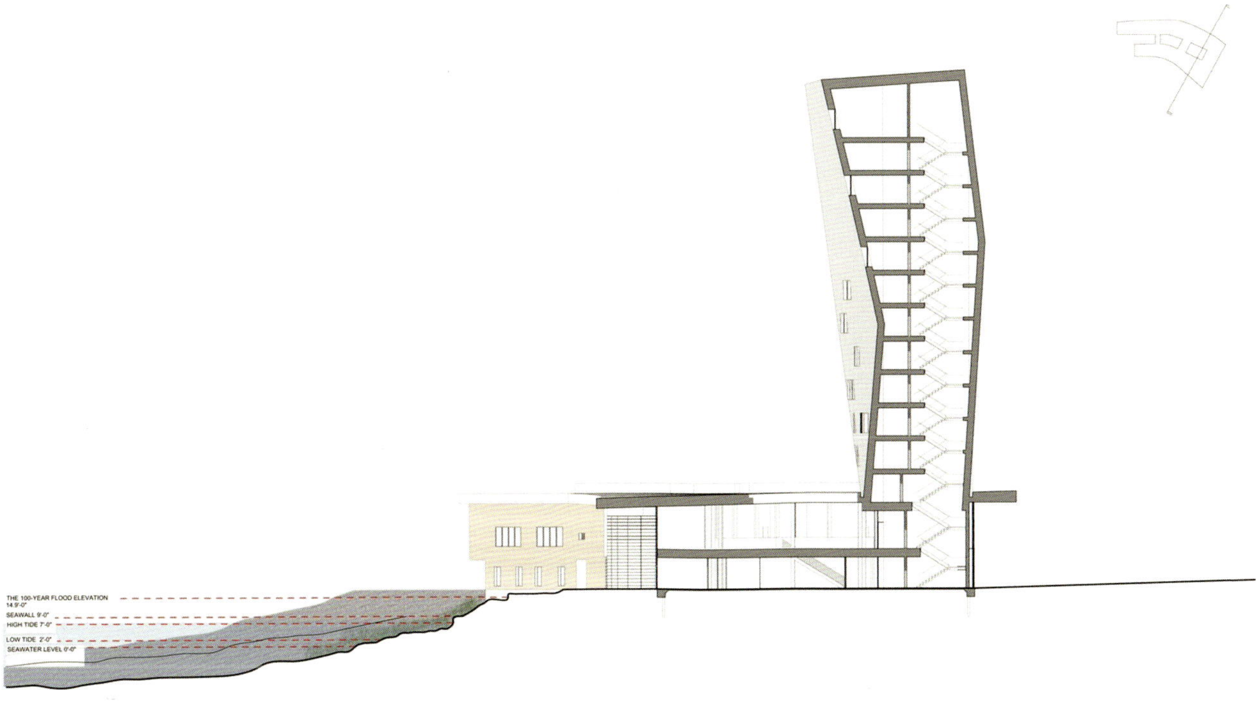
THE 100-YEAR FLOOD ELEVATION
14.9'-0"
SEAWALL 9'-0"
HIGH TIDE 7'-0"
LOW TIDE 2'-0"
SEAWATER LEVEL 0'-0"

03

RESIDENTIAL TOWER
LABORATORY
ADMIN & ACADEMIC CENTER
COMMUNITY OUTREACH
PRIVATE
semi-
PUBLIC
PUBLIC

04

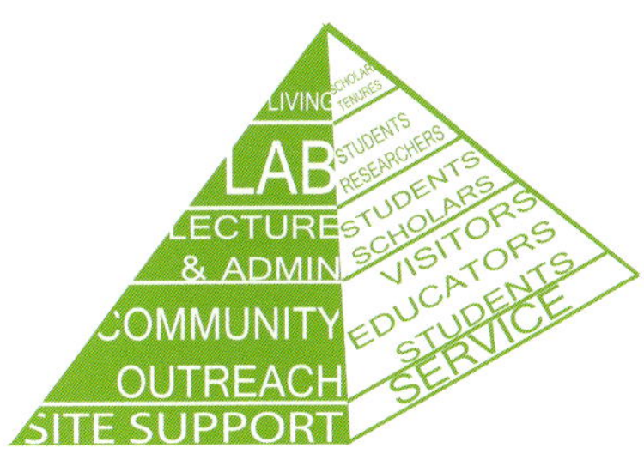
LIVING
LAB
LECTURE
& ADMIN
COMMUNITY
OUTREACH
SITE SUPPORT
SCHOLARS TENURES
STUDENTS RESEARCHERS
STUDENTS SCHOLARS
VISITORS
EDUCATORS
STUDENTS
SERVICE

05

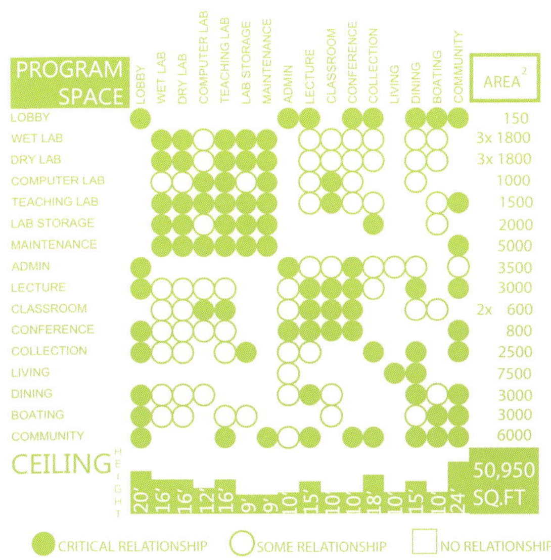
PROGRAM SPACE
LOBBY
WET LAB
DRY LAB
COMPUTER LAB
TEACHING LAB
LAB STORAGE
MAINTENANCE
ADMIN
LECTURE
CLASSROOM
CONFERENCE
COLLECTION
LIVING
DINING
BOATING
COMMUNITY
AREA²
150
3x 1800
3x 1800
1000
1500
2000
5000
3500
3000
2x 600
800
2500
7500
3000
3000
6000
CEILING HEIGHT
20'
16'
16'
12'
16'
9'
9'
10'
15'
10'
10'
18'
10'
15'
10'
24'
50,950 SQ.FT
CRITICAL RELATIONSHIP
SOME RELATIONSHIP
NO RELATIONSHIP

06

01

02

03

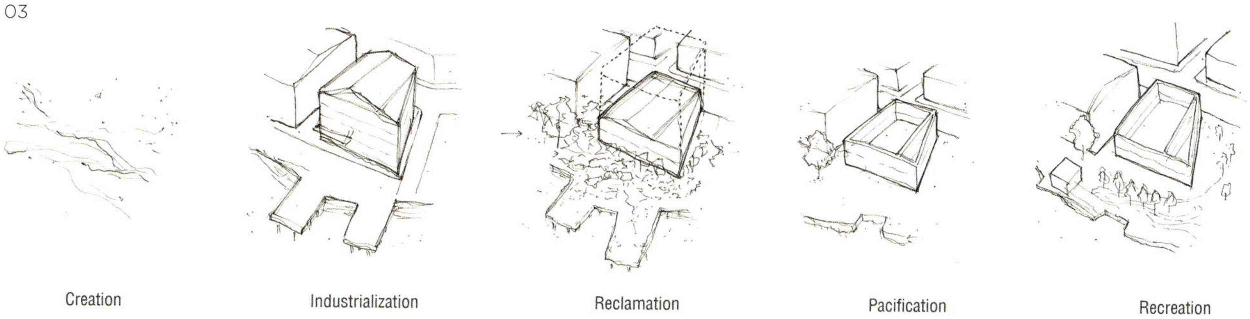

04

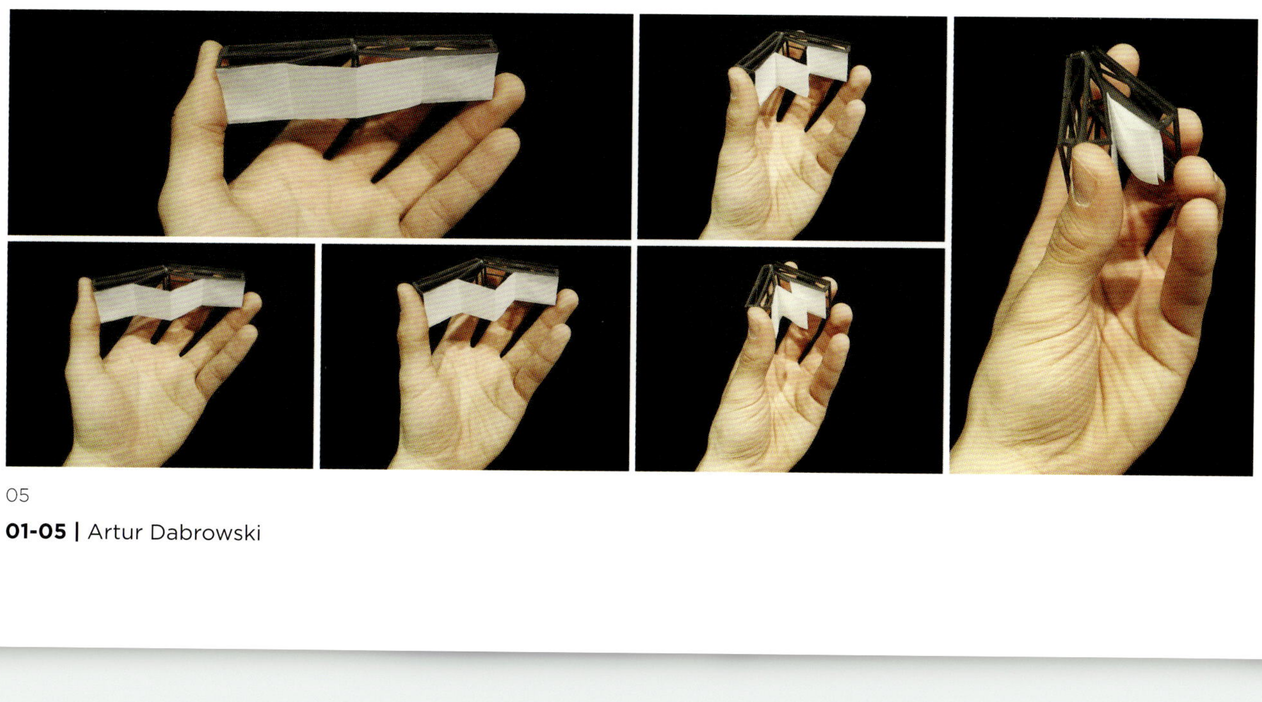

05

01-05 | Artur Dabrowski

01

02

03

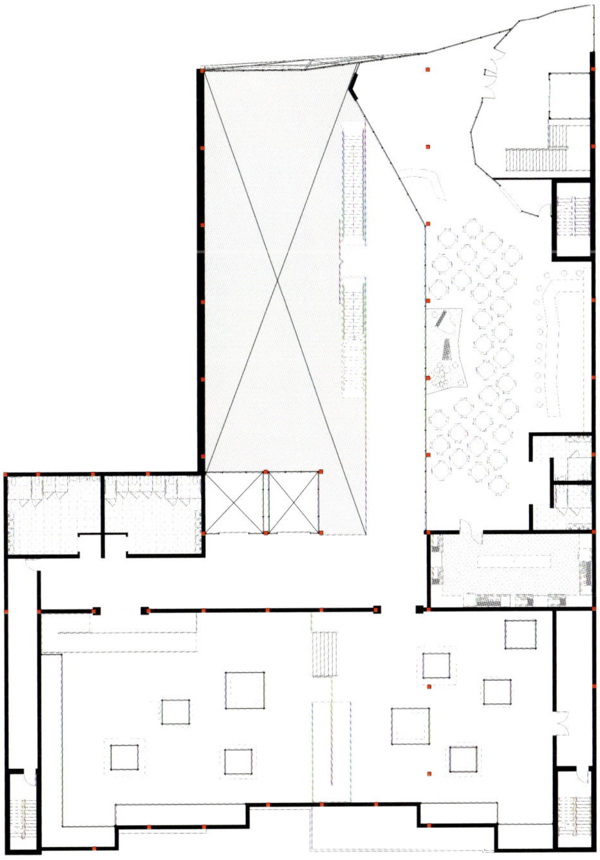

04

01-04 | Michael McPartland

MAST

OF ARCHITECTURE

ER

1st SEMESTER DESIGN

FACULTY
Bradley Horn / Babak Bryan

The Master of Architecture Program is an intensive three-year course of study progressing from fundamental to advanced education in architectural theory and practice. The studio sequence is composed of a four semester core taught by our full-time faculty and two advanced studios taught by visiting distinguished critics from outside of the school who bring their own unique research to the classroom.

The first semester is an introduction to architectural theory, drawing and model making. A series of problems teach students how to develop a critical relationship to space, form, program, diagramming, digital technology & orthographic projection. In the second semester students are introduced to the urban context and address a series of problems that focus on structural, environmental, material, code and zoning systems. The third semester focuses on building systems integration, structural systems and technical documentation. In this comprehensive design studio students develop a building from schematic design through the construction documents phase. The final studio in the four semester core focuses on sustainable housing. Here emphasis is placed on the research of urban and building precedents as well as on the use of environmental modeling and visualization tools to measure and integrate complex data into housing solutions.

This fall Visiting Distinguished critics Joe Tanney and John Hong both took on a branch library in East Harlem. In the spring, Yolande Daniels addressed the relocation of Essex Street Market in Manhattan's Lower East Side, while Audrey Matlock challenged her students with the design of a museum on the Karakoy waterfront in Istanbul.

Bradley Horn
First Year Design Coordinator

Katerina Marcelja
BRADLEY HORN, CRITIC

01

03

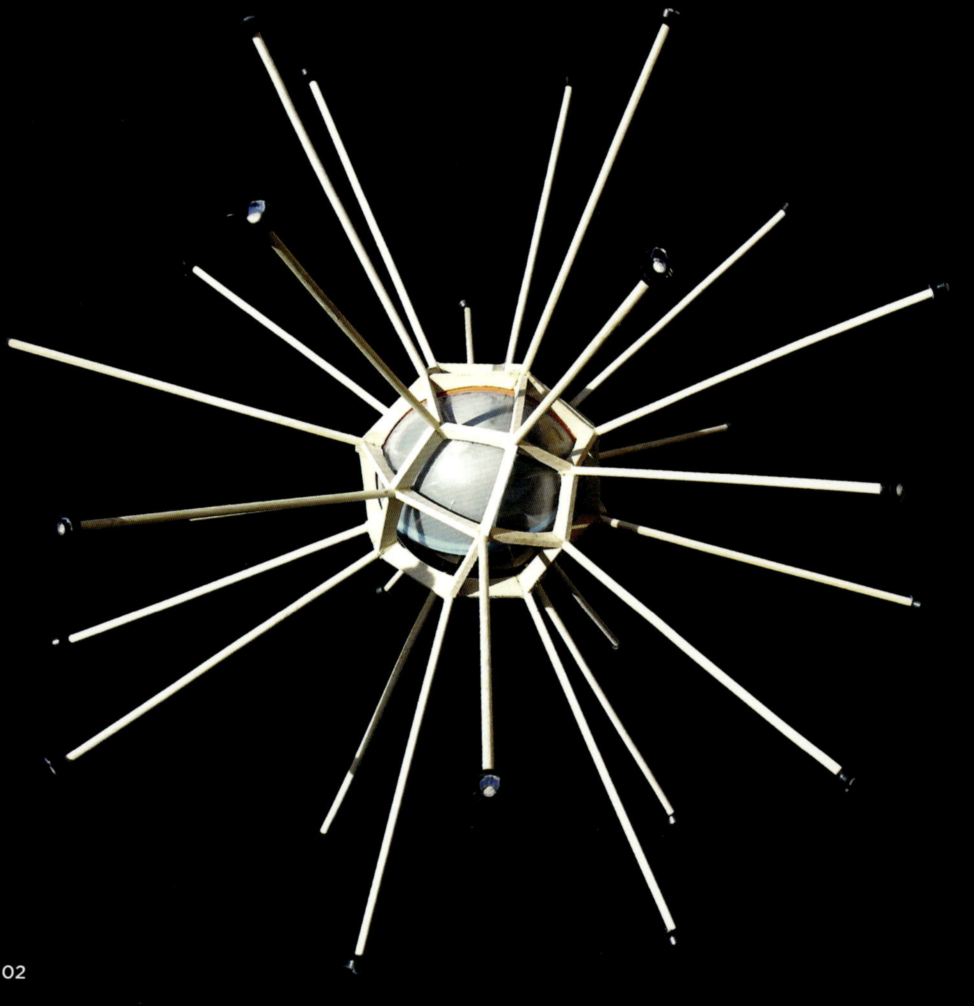

02

04

05

06

01 | Brian Lantz
02 | Benjamin Tulman
03 | Katerina Marcelja / Ahmed Dirhalleh
04 | Salvatore Cosenza
05 | Maura Whang / Brian Lantz
06 | Jennifer Ewald

01

02

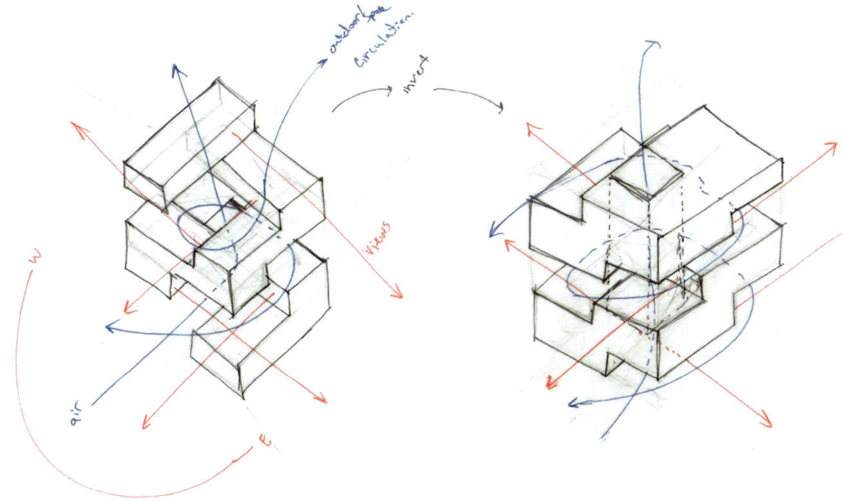

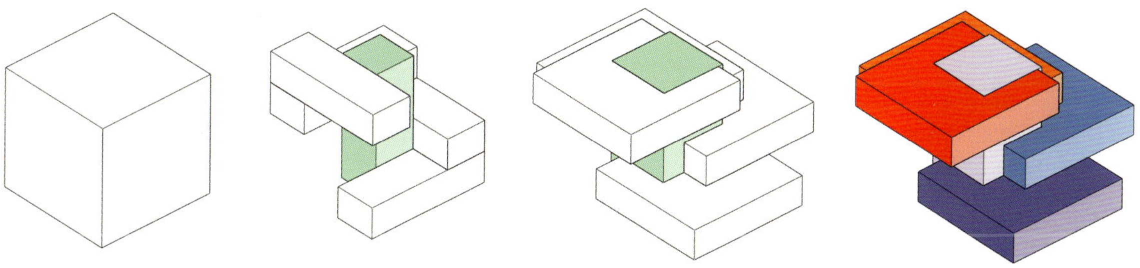

03

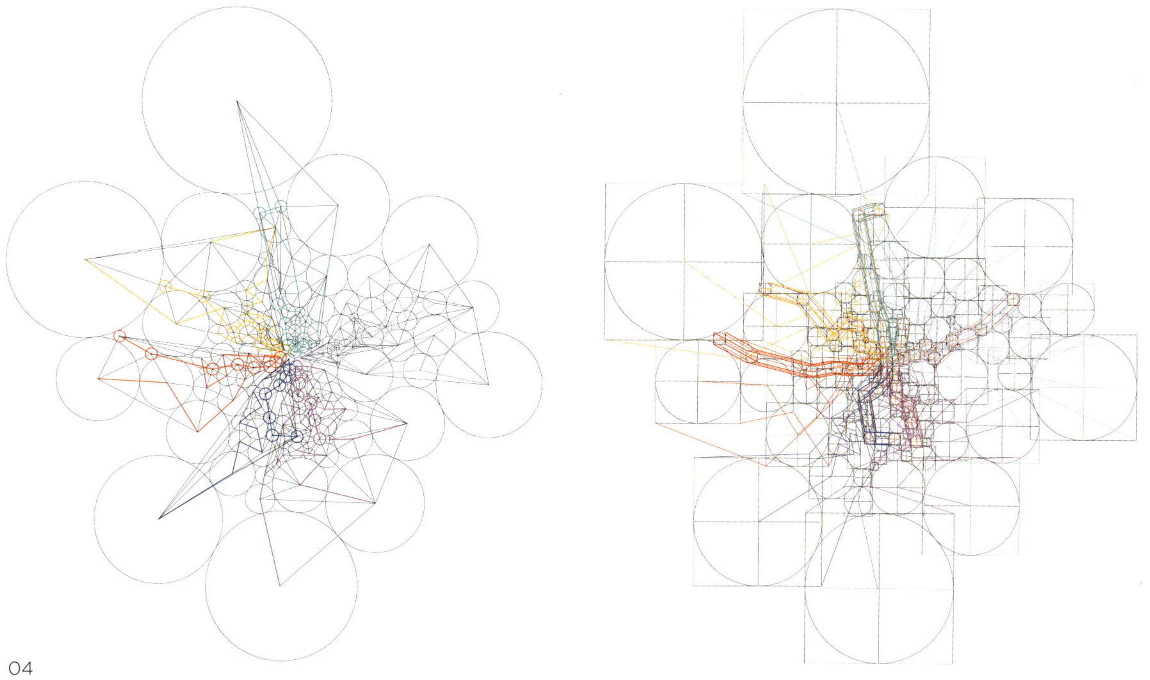

04

01, 02 | Michael Joseph
03 | Nagi Alamri / Ronald Martin
04 | Adelaida Baez-Urena

2nd SEMESTER DESIGN

FACULTY
Bradley Horn / Elisabetta Terragni

Under the title "Reduce, Reuse, Recycle," this spring students were challenged with three exercises of increasing scale and complexity focusing on structural, environmental, material, code and zoning systems respectively. The first problem introduced students to intuitive structural behavior through the design and construction of a freestanding wall made out of recycled and readily available materials. The second problem partnered students with a structural engineer to re-imagine the BMW Guggenheim Lab in NYC; a temporary pavilion used as an urban think tank, community center and public gathering space in Manhattan's East Village. Students designed structural systems for the pavilion, invented programmatic possibilities for its use and, in partnership with First Street Green, exhibited their proposals as part of the New Museum's Ideas City Festival in April 2013. In collaboration with the Harlem School of Arts (HSA) and the J. Max Bond Center on Design for the Just City, the final project of the semester asked students to redesign and expand the existing HSA black box theater as a way of strengthening the school's civic presence within the broader community. Students were asked to synthesize the acoustical challenges of the program type, the functional complexities associated with designing a multi-use performance venue and the less tangible memories which lay dormant within the geological and social layers of the site.

Bradley Horn
Director, Master of Architecture Program

Michael Joseph
BRADLEY HORN, CRITIC

01

02

03

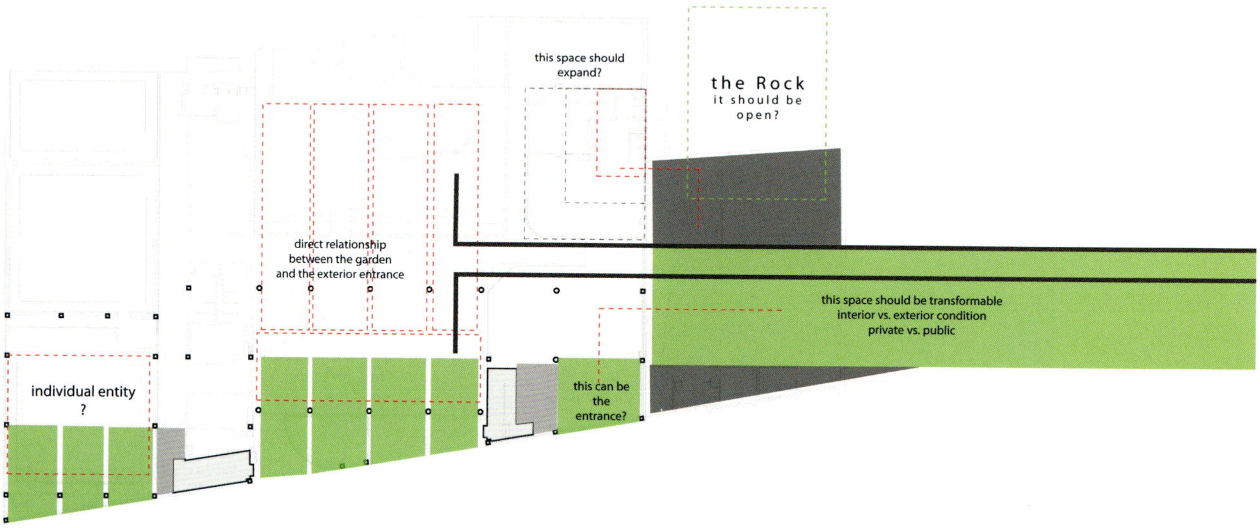
this space should expand?
the Rock
it should be open?
direct relationship between the garden and the exterior entrance
this space should be transformable
interior vs. exterior condition
private vs. public
individual entity ?
this can be the entrance?

04

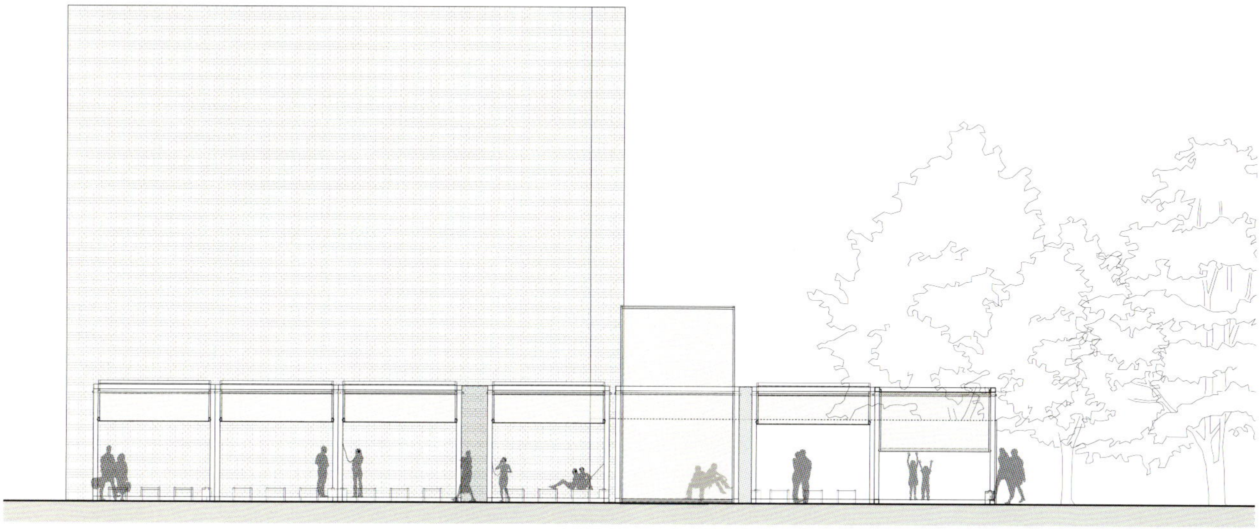

05

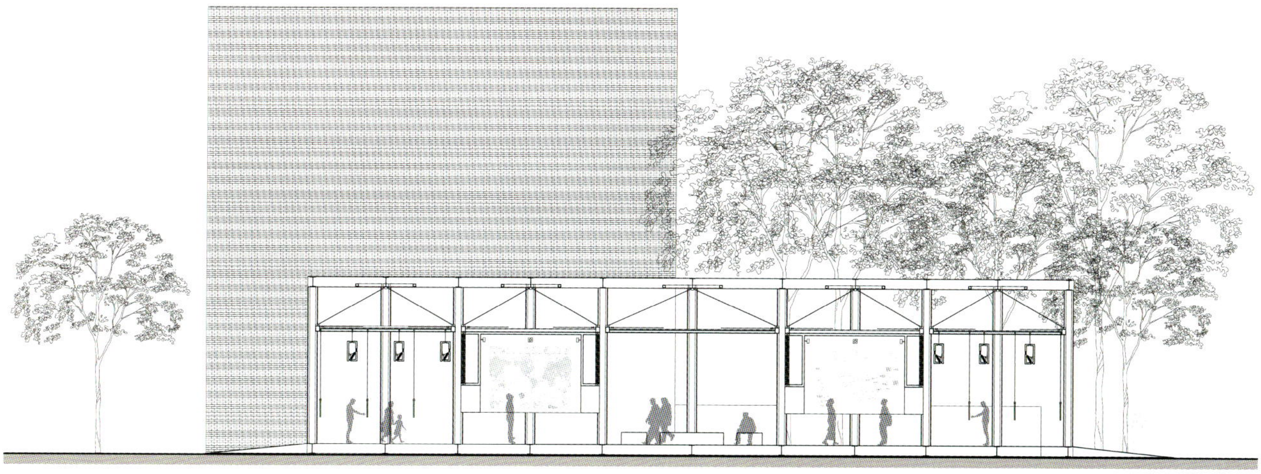

06

07

01 | Mohammed Tammam Munir
02 | Alexander La Ferla
03 | Christina Hernandez
04, 06 | Adelaida Baez-Urena
05 | Ronald Martin
07 | Paola Martinez

01

02

03

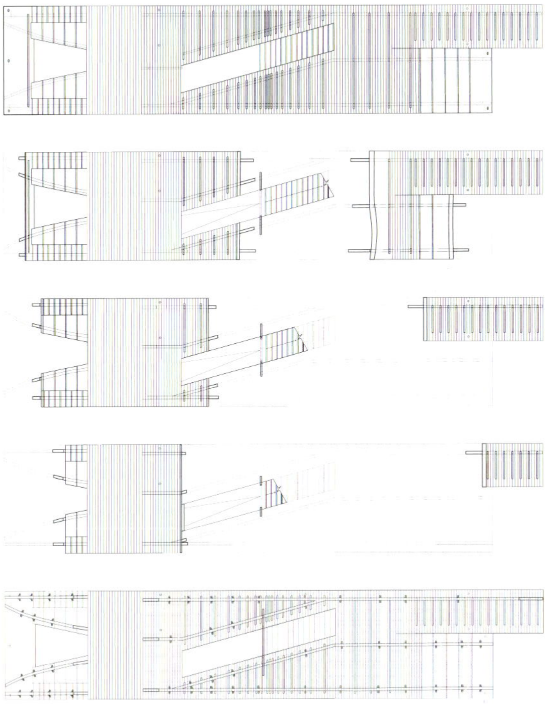

04

05

06

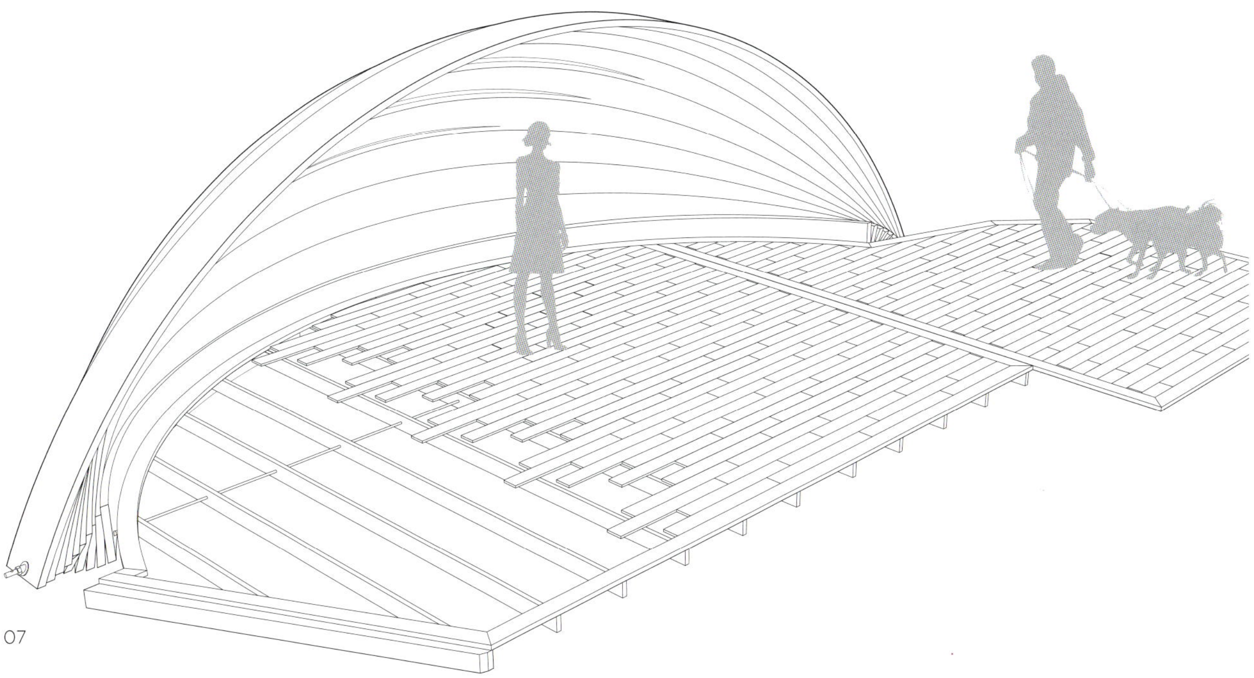

07

01 | Jill Bunyea
02 | Katerina Marcelja
03 | Salvatore Cosenza
04 | Jennifer Ewald
05 | Benjamin Tulman
06 | Nicholas Friedmann
07 | Brian Lantz

3rd SEMESTER DESIGN

FACULTY
Ali Hocek / Martin Stigsgaard

ON DEMAND
Affordable On-demand Office Space in New York City.

As the economy of the United States continues its struggle to return to previous levels of well-being, the need to look at alternate means of finding and developing work is essential to the survival of the individual and small businesses.

The projects in the studio investigate a new building typology for ground-up on-demand workspaces. The projects define a symbiotic concept where on-demand activities generate revenue to sustain the running cost of the building, provide efficient and competitive spaces, and increased interaction among significant activities in and around the building. Students consider overlaps and proximities to differing and divergent program elements for both their social interactive qualities, and as architecturally charged spaces. Aesthetically, the building is its own signage and promotion.

The project is developed in four phases of pre-design, schematic design, design development, and construction documents. The last phase is based on required building permits of the Building Department. Throughout the semester the students develop their designs working with a structural and HVAC engineer, landscape architect, lighting designer, curtain wall/building envelope specialist, specification writer, and cost estimator. During the first month, the consultants present an overview of their professional requirements, as well as specifics for the students' projects, in a symposium.

Ali Hocek and Martin Stigsgaard
Third Semester Design Coordinators

Stephanie Paul / Timea Hopp
ALI HOCEK, CRITIC

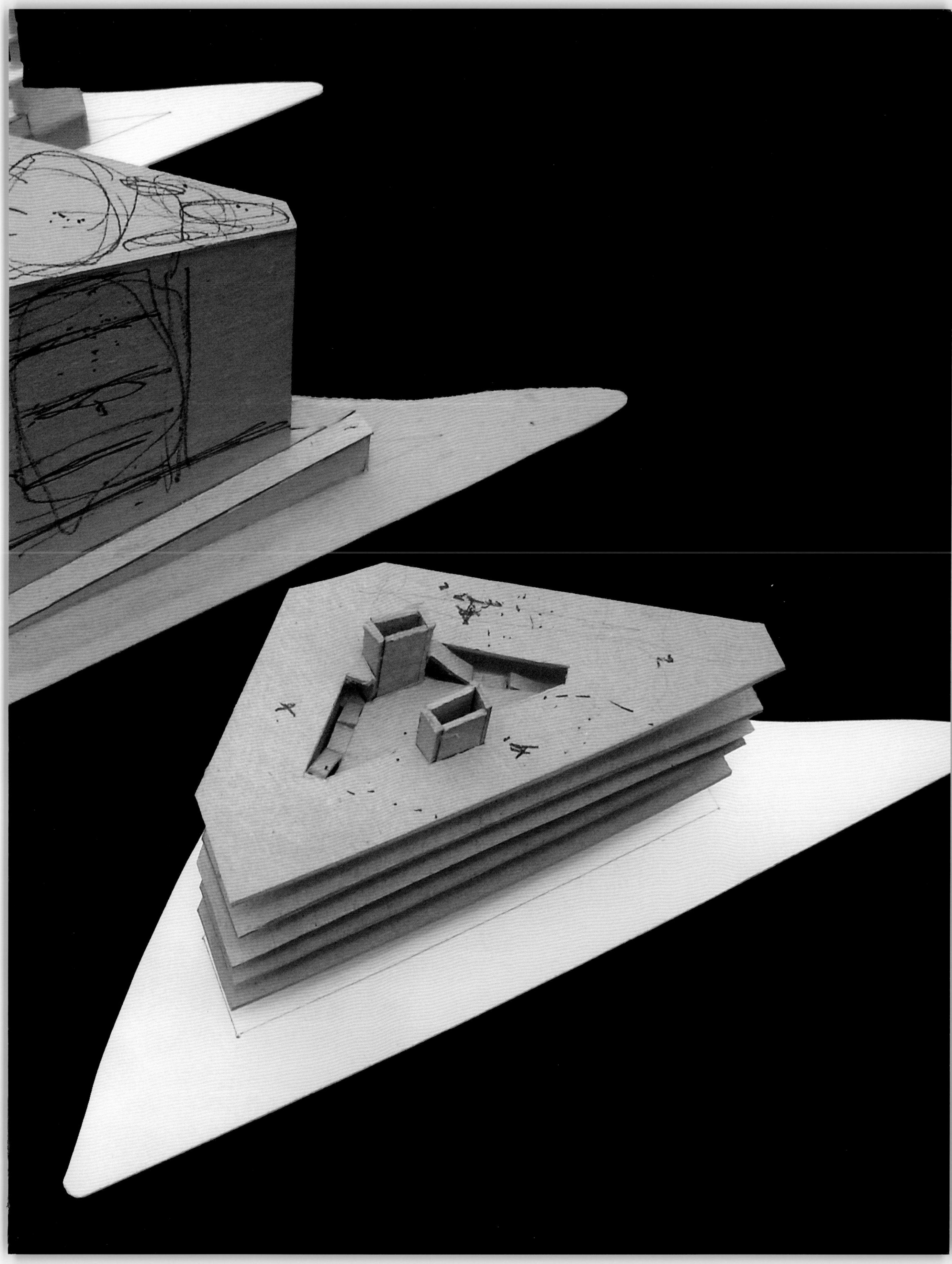

01

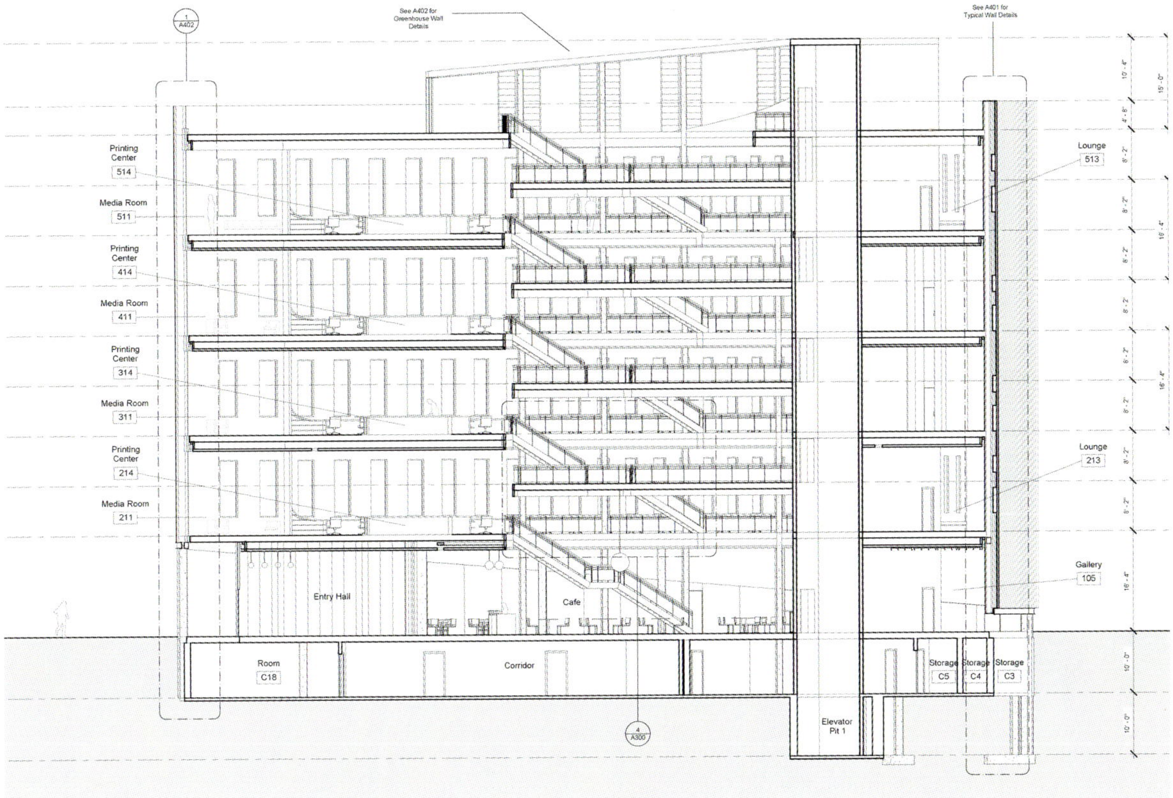

02

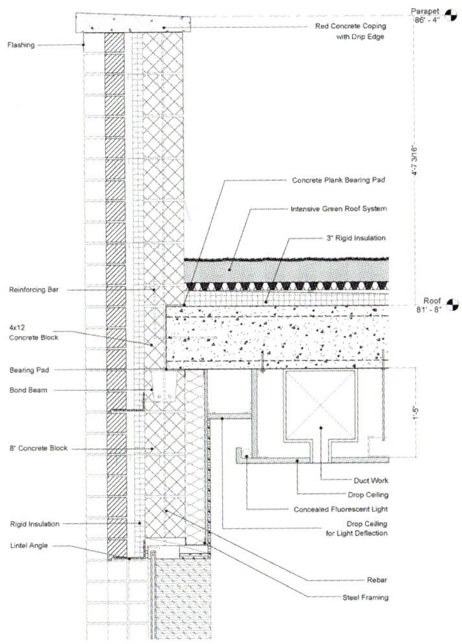

03

04

01 | Hillary Zhao / Daniel Brown
02, 03 | Stephanie Paul / Timea Hopp
04 | Bryant Stanton / Ross Levine

DUNKIN' DONUTS

01

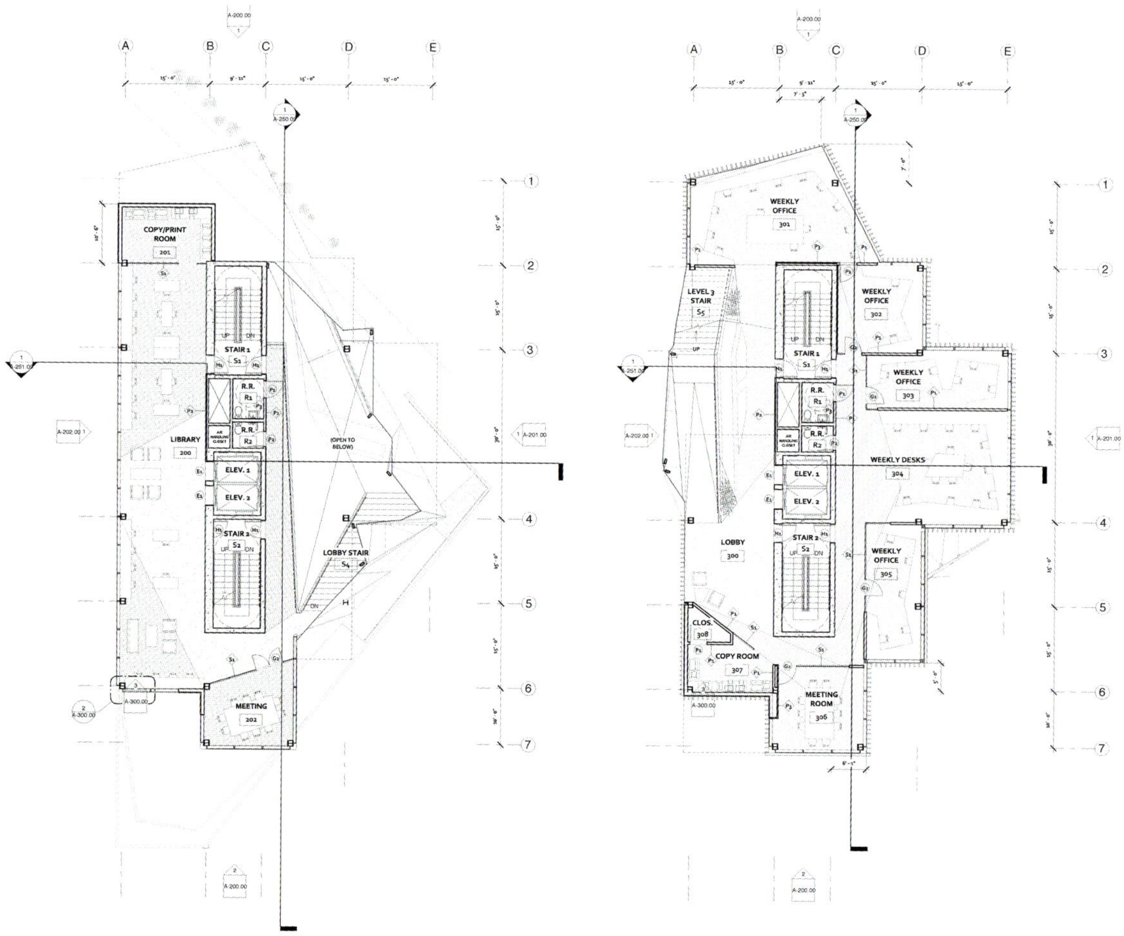
COPY/PRINT ROOM
201
LIBRARY
200
STAIR 1
STAIR 2
ELEV. 1
ELEV. 2
(OPEN TO BELOW)
LOBBY STAIR
MEETING
202
WEEKLY OFFICE
301
LEVEL 3 STAIR
WEEKLY OFFICE
302
WEEKLY OFFICE
303
WEEKLY DESKS
304
LOBBY
300
WEEKLY OFFICE
305
COPY ROOM
307
MEETING ROOM
306

02

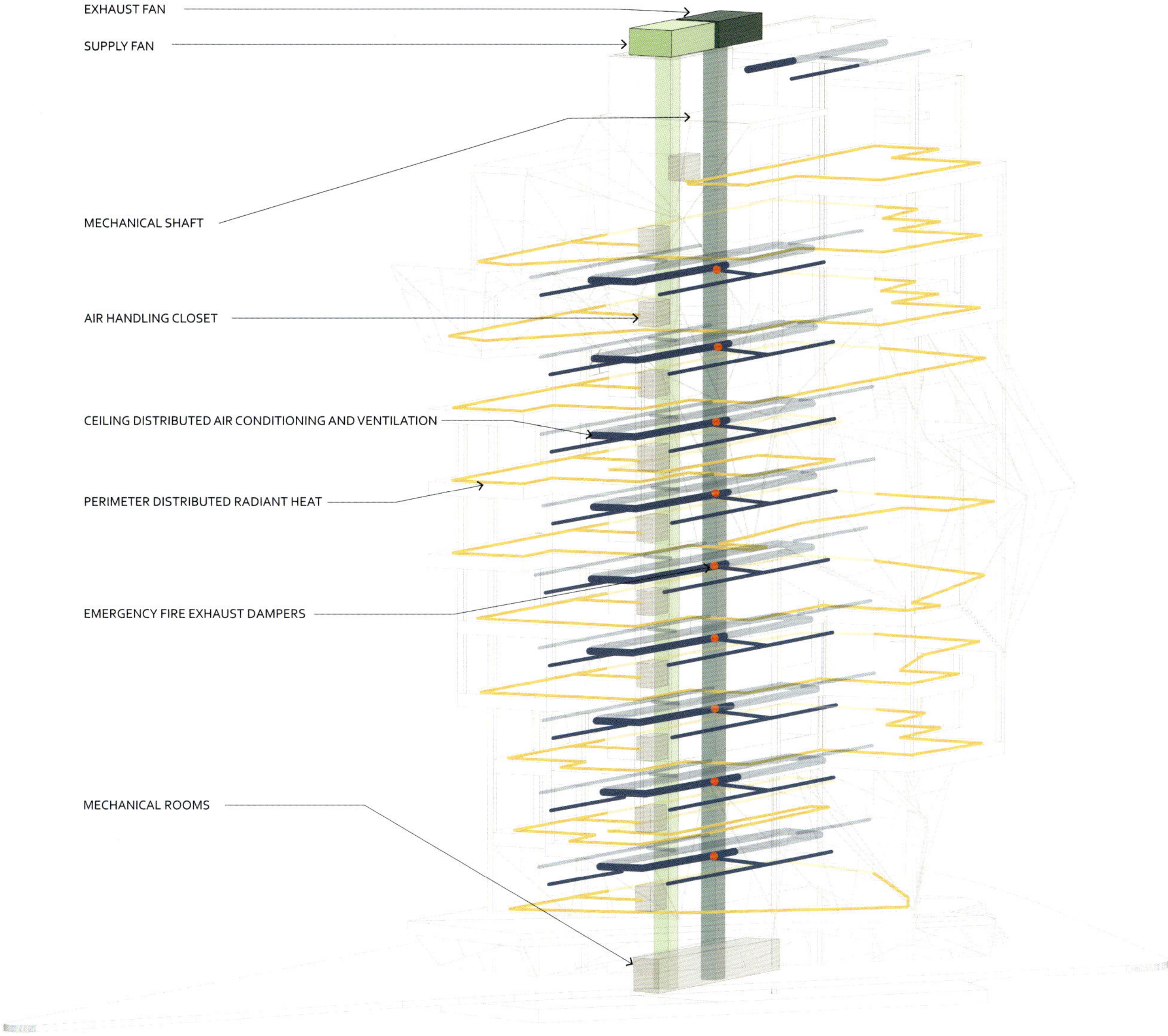

03

01-04 | Rebecca Dorff / Anna Struthers

04

4th SEMESTER DESIGN

FACULTY
Julio Salcedo-Fernandez / Yehre Suh

The purpose of the studio is to provide a cross-disciplinary platform to expand the efficacy of design disciplines in relation to contemporary environmental predicaments and urbanization trends. As we think about landscape and architecture vis-à-vis settlement, the role and density of the urban environment and its relation to its encompassing ecosystems are among the most salient issues. To this end, the studio as a whole will examine the layered site of Elizabeth NJ. We will be focusing particularly on the areas adjacent to the Elizabeth River bordering the downtown and adjacent to the train station. Landscape and architecture students will collaborate to produce nuanced and daring neighborhood proposals that uncover the operational systems and logics at a variety of scales from the regional to the immediate. These proposals will have the program of Housing as their key architectural component. Housing will be the complementary topic of the architectural studio. Above all the studio seeks a deep understanding of the motivations and procedures of each discipline as means to further the design and shared pedagogical intents.

Julio Salcedo-Fernandez
Fourth Semester Design Coordinator

Bryant Stanton / Ross Levine
JULIO SALCEDO-FERNANDEZ, CRITIC

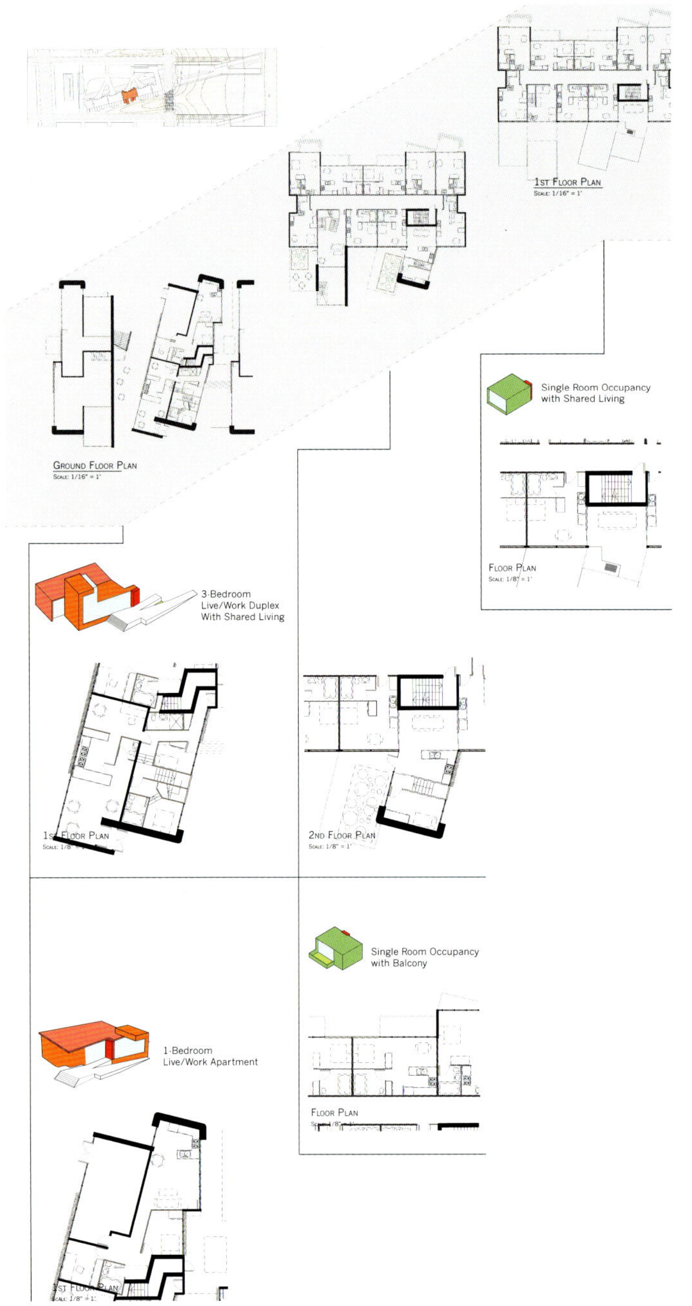

01

Scaled Living

Waste not want not. Diversity of units and living arrangements pools resources, provides connectivity and enables all tenants to find the right-sized unit

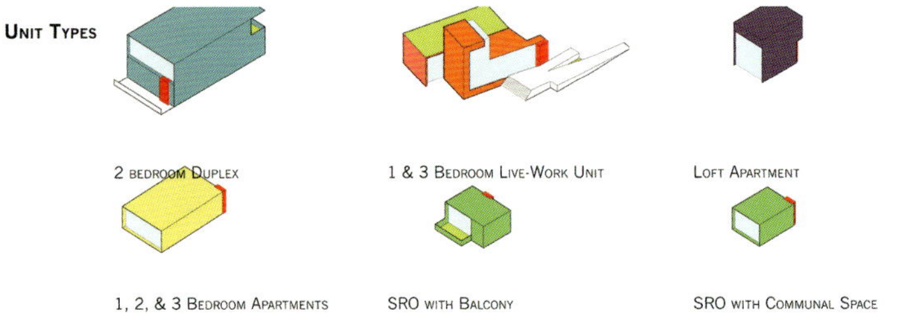

02

03

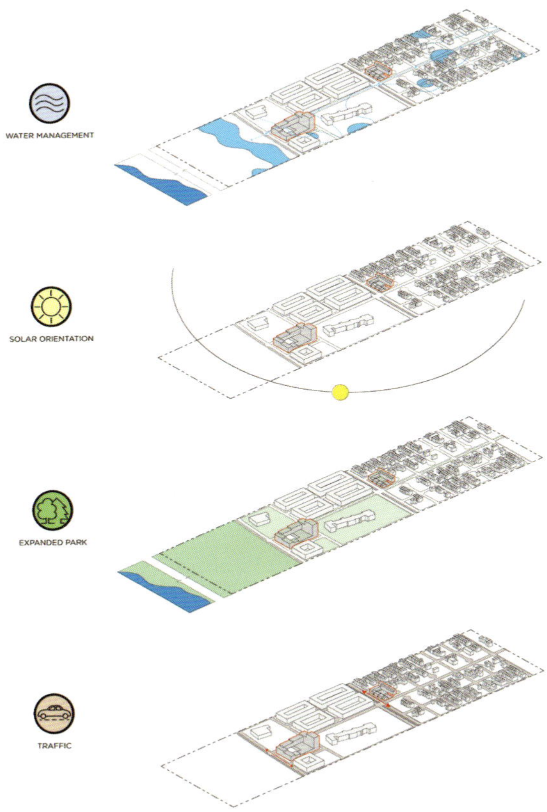

04

05

01, 02 | Michele Flournoy / Daniel Cassidy
03-05 | Bryant Stanton / Ross Levine

01

02

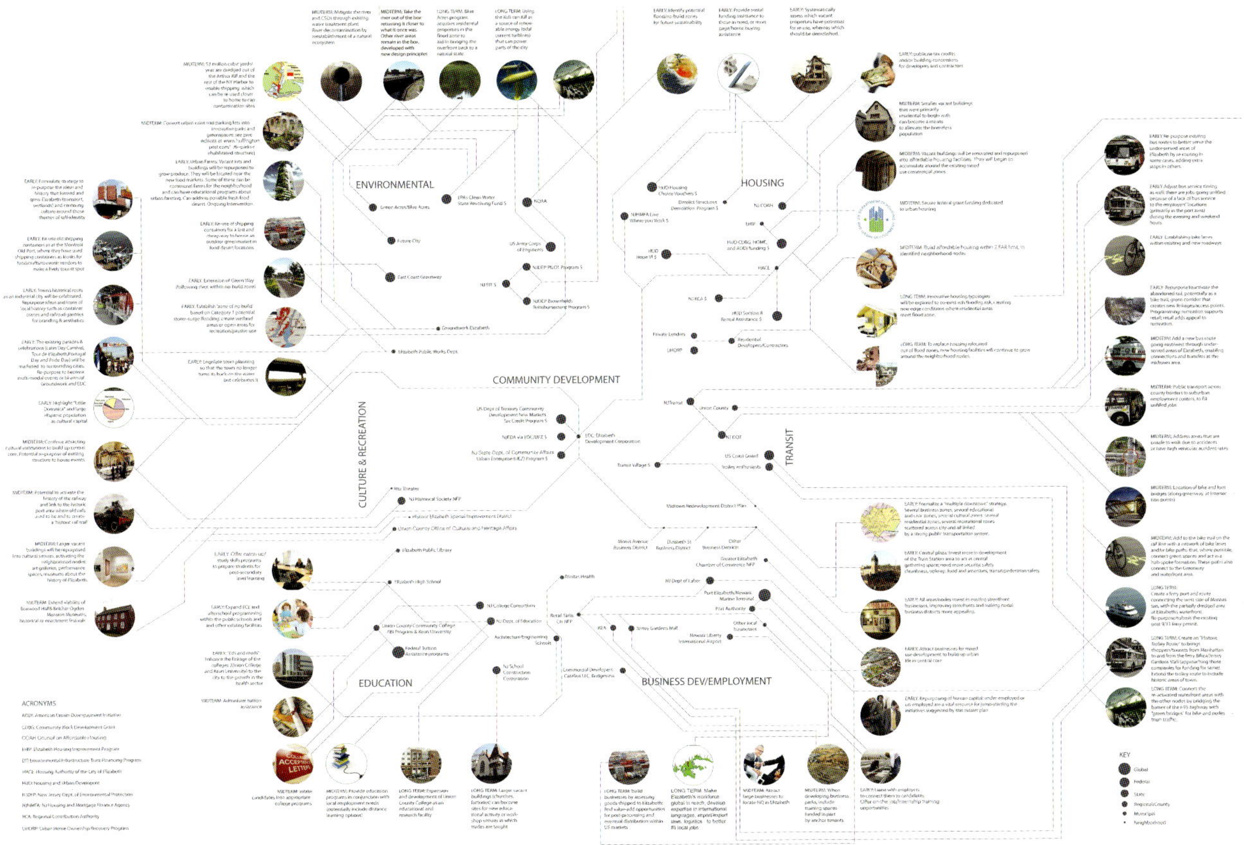

03

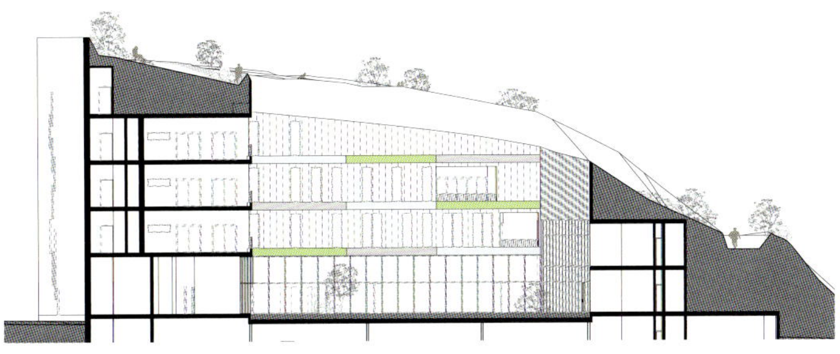

04

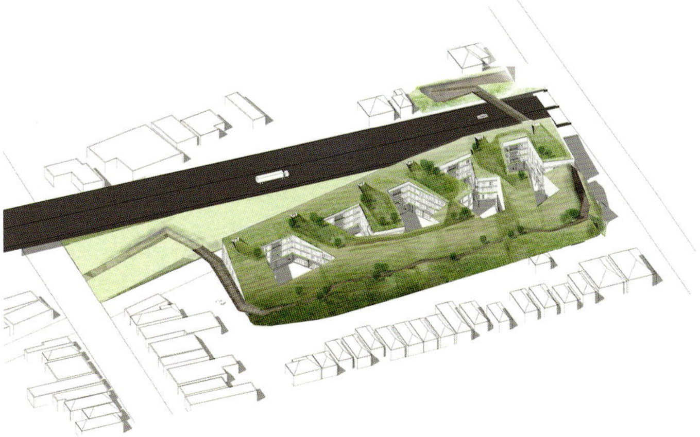

05

01, 02 | Rebecca Dorff / Shelley Yang
03-05 | Claire Ross / Kristen Cowan

5th SEMESTER DESIGN

FACULTY
John Hong / Joseph Tanney

A BRANCH LIBRARY FOR EAST HARLEM

One of the most iconic public building types, the library has been central to the life of the city in both its elevated and everyday roles. Both a repository of knowledge and a community meeting ground, it has the potential to both form the city around it and be in-formed by its context. Although central libraries have typically been conceived as iconic public edifices, what is the role of the smaller scale branch library?

Through a series of iterative and multi-scale diagrams, drawings, and models, the thesis arguments took on strategic weight using representation not as merely a way to passively describe the project, but to actively inscribe the work with conceptual potency.

John Hong
Visiting Distinguished Critic

Taylor Harper
JOHN HONG, CRITIC

01

02

03

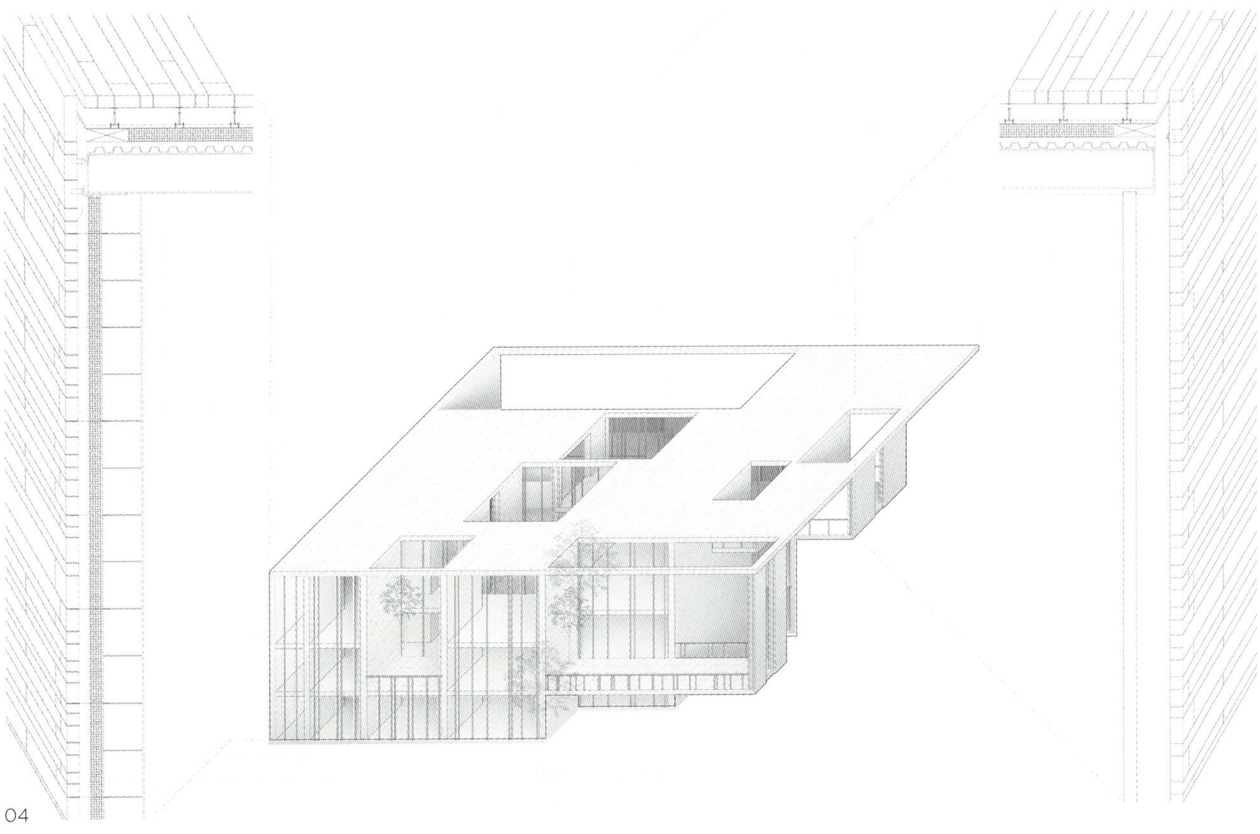

04

01, 02 | Taylor Harper
03, 04 | Juliet Ingber

01

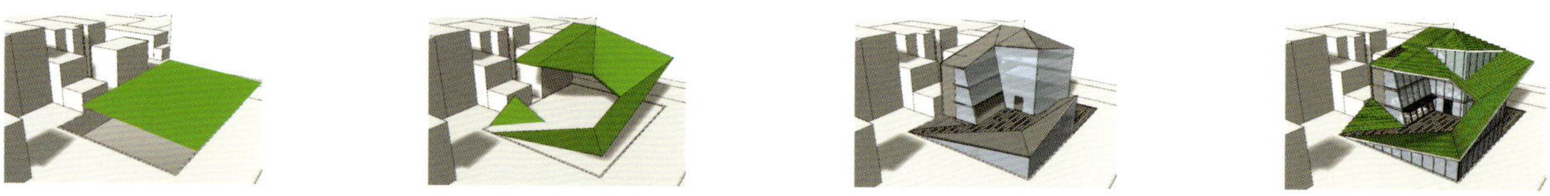

02

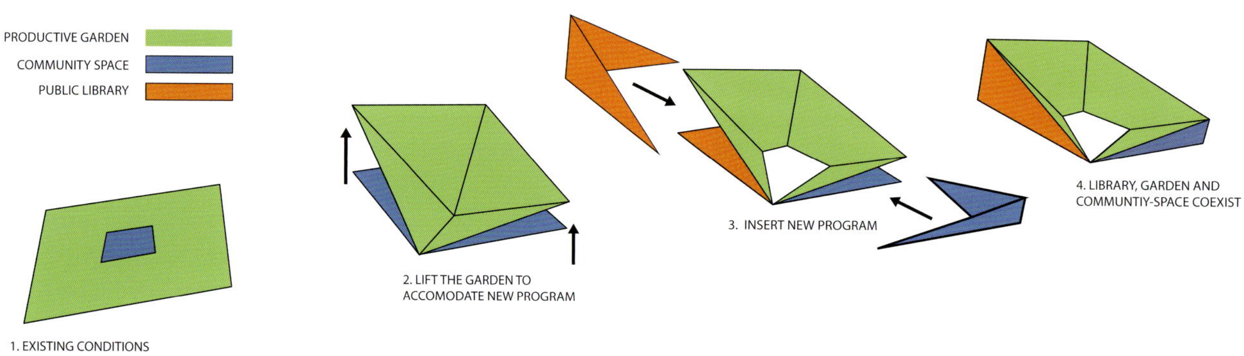
PRODUCTIVE GARDEN
COMMUNITY SPACE
PUBLIC LIBRARY
1. EXISTING CONDITIONS
2. LIFT THE GARDEN TO
ACCOMODATE NEW PROGRAM
3. INSERT NEW PROGRAM
4. LIBRARY, GARDEN AND
COMMUNTIY-SPACE COEXIST

03

04

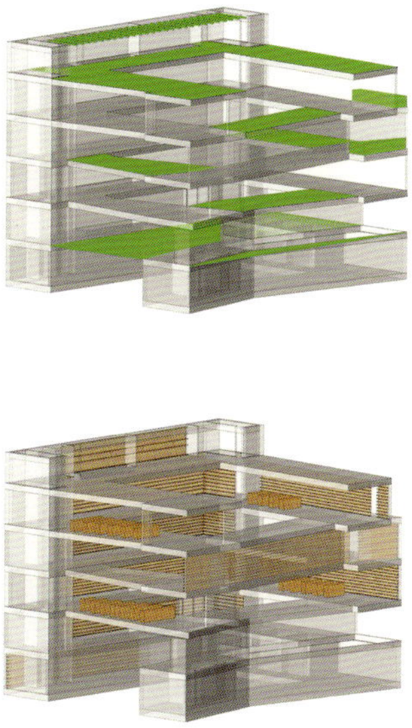

05

06

01-03 | Michael Luft-Weissberg
04-06 | Meagan Pauley

6th SEMESTER DESIGN

FACULTY
Yolande Daniels / Audrey Matlock

On the Karakoy waterfront in Istanbul, this studio jointly investigated the impact on urban development to the city and a building to a specific site.

Located at the intersection of the Sea of Marmara, Bosphorus Strait and the Golden Horn, the site occupies an important location along possibly the most legendary east/west trade route.

With the recent abandonment of Karakoy shipping facilities, the city is currently leaving the fate of this area to individual development interests intent on building shopping malls.

Based on individual research, each student developed a counter proposal to re-envision the site in a way to bring lasting value to the city; following this each developed a specific building program and a comprehensive museum building design.

Audrey Matlock
Visiting Distinguished Critic

Michael Luft-Weissberg
YOLANDE DANIELS, CRITIC

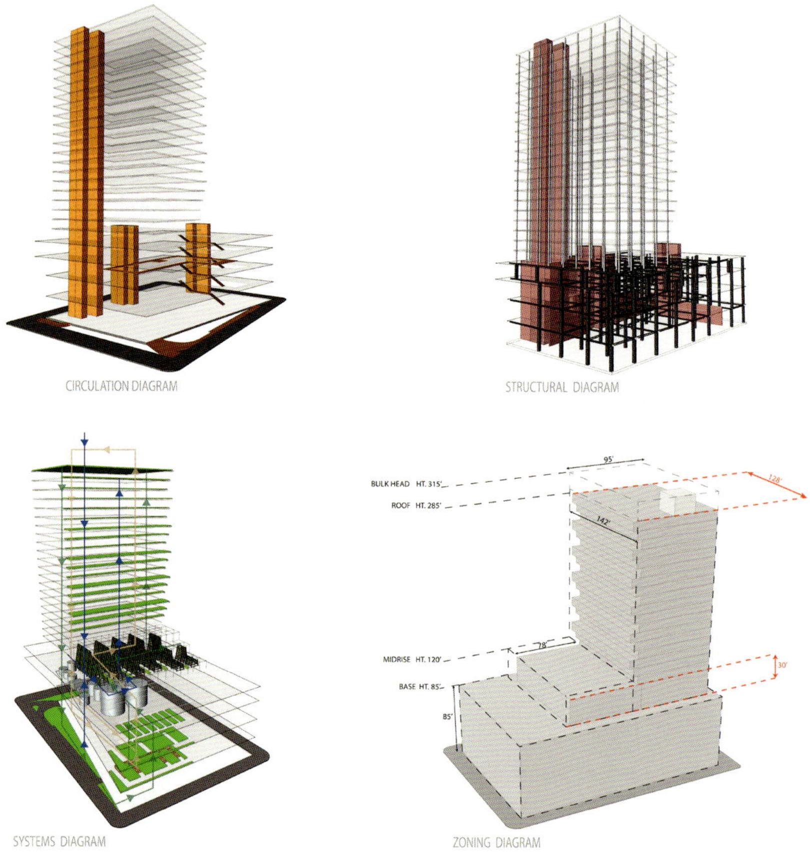
CIRCULATION DIAGRAM
STRUCTURAL DIAGRAM
SYSTEMS DIAGRAM
BULK HEAD HT. 315'
ROOF HT. 285'
95'
128'
142'
78'
MIDRISE HT. 120'
BASE HT. 85'
85'
30'
ZONING DIAGRAM

01

02

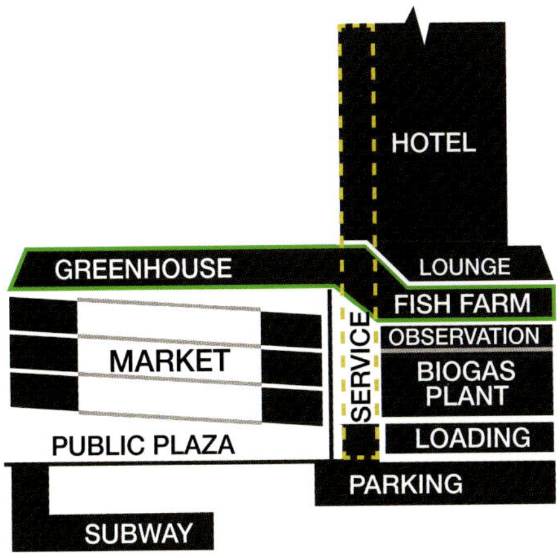

03

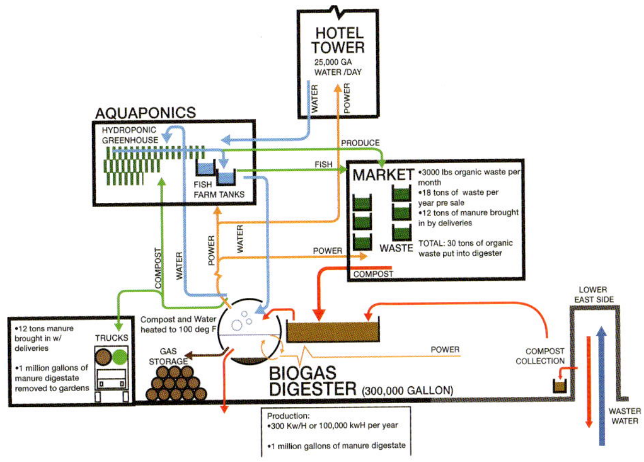

04

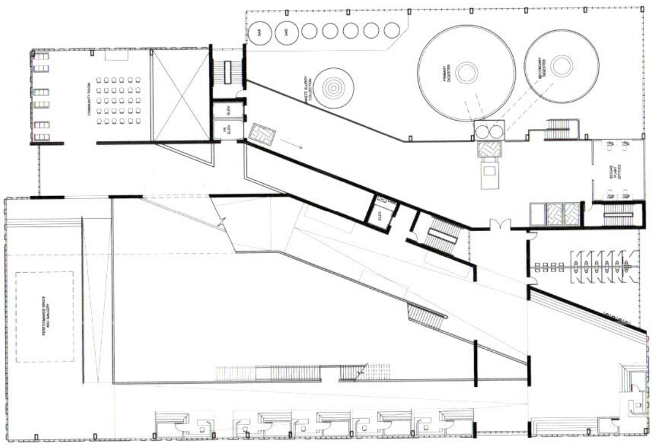

05

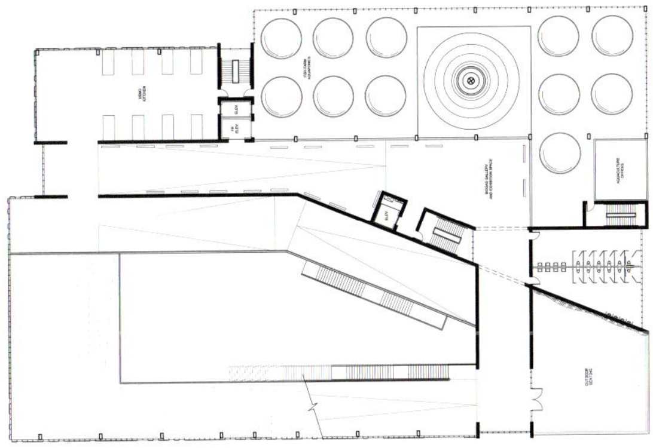

06

07

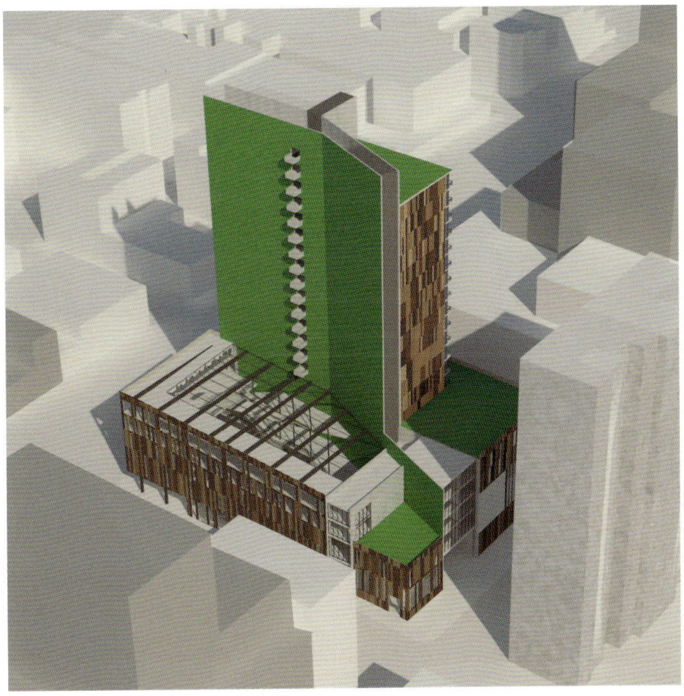

08

01, 02 | Meagan Pauley
03-08 | Michael Luft-Weissberg

01

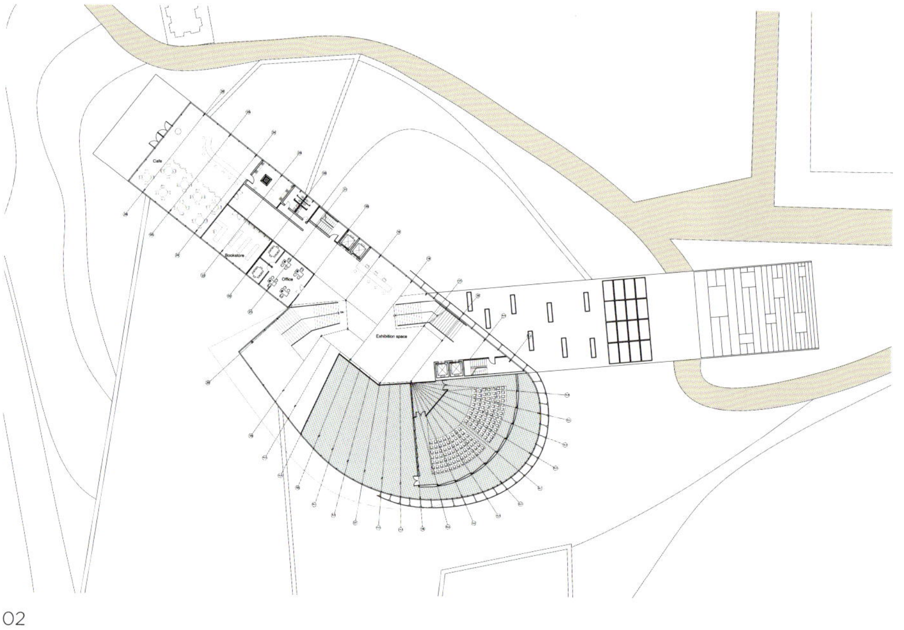

02

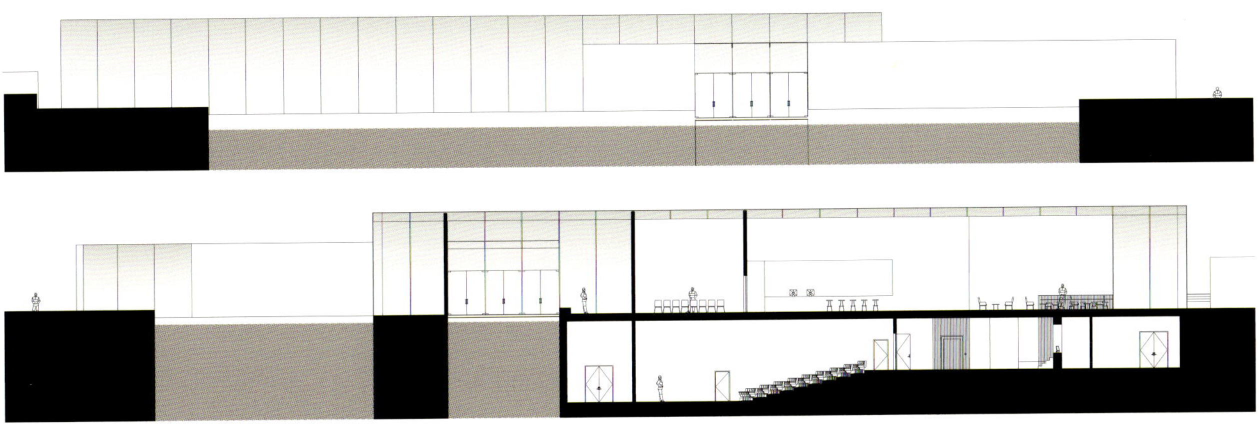

03

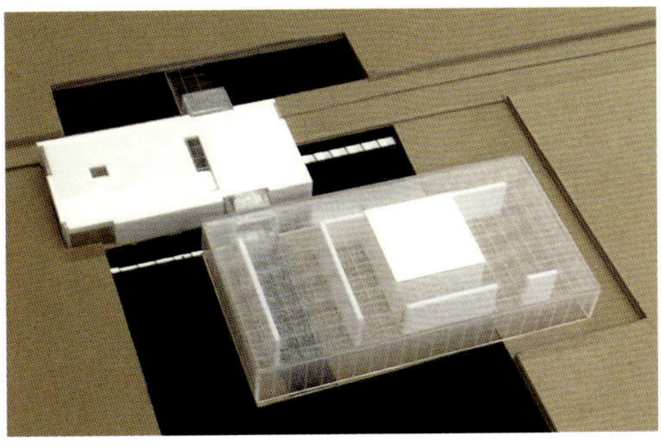

04

01, 02 | Francesca Bucci Vernizzi
03, 04 | Taylor Harper

MAST

OF URBAN DESIGN

ER

1st and 2nd SEMESTER DESIGN

FACULTY
Michael Sorkin

We began the year, as is our wont, with a limbering-up exercise: the design of an imaginary city, an Urbanagram. Working together on the basis of a series of sequentially disclosed instructions, students built and enhanced a very large model. The bulk of the term was devoted to individual investigations of a New York City site, Willets Point. Currently the home of a dense and funky ecology of automobile repair shops, the site adjoins CitiField, downtown Flushing, and Flushing Meadows Corona Park, and is walled by a tangle of major expressways and transit lines. Like much of coastal New York, it is highly threatened by the rising waters of climate change. Long coveted for generic development - including big box stores - the site holds great promise for more imaginative and sustainable solutions of which students suggested many.

The second semester launched with our annual trip, this year to Tianjin, China, the seaport for Beijing. The weather was cruelly cold and that entire area was in the throes of a toxic crisis: breathing was a challenge. We nevertheless persevered and, with the assistance of colleagues from the School of Architecture at Tianjin University, investigated a coastal site subject to massive expansion pressures, including a huge enlargement of the harbor. Students invented and designed their own sites, which ranged from interventions along the waterfront, to projects that looked to counter the immense pressures for sprawl by focusing on village and town renewal, to designs for the entire region. Each, however, examined the implications of his or her research at a variety of scales with a variety of urban forms and systems in mind.

Michael Sorkin
Director, Master of Urban Design Program

Carlos Rodriguez
MICHAEL SORKIN, CRITIC

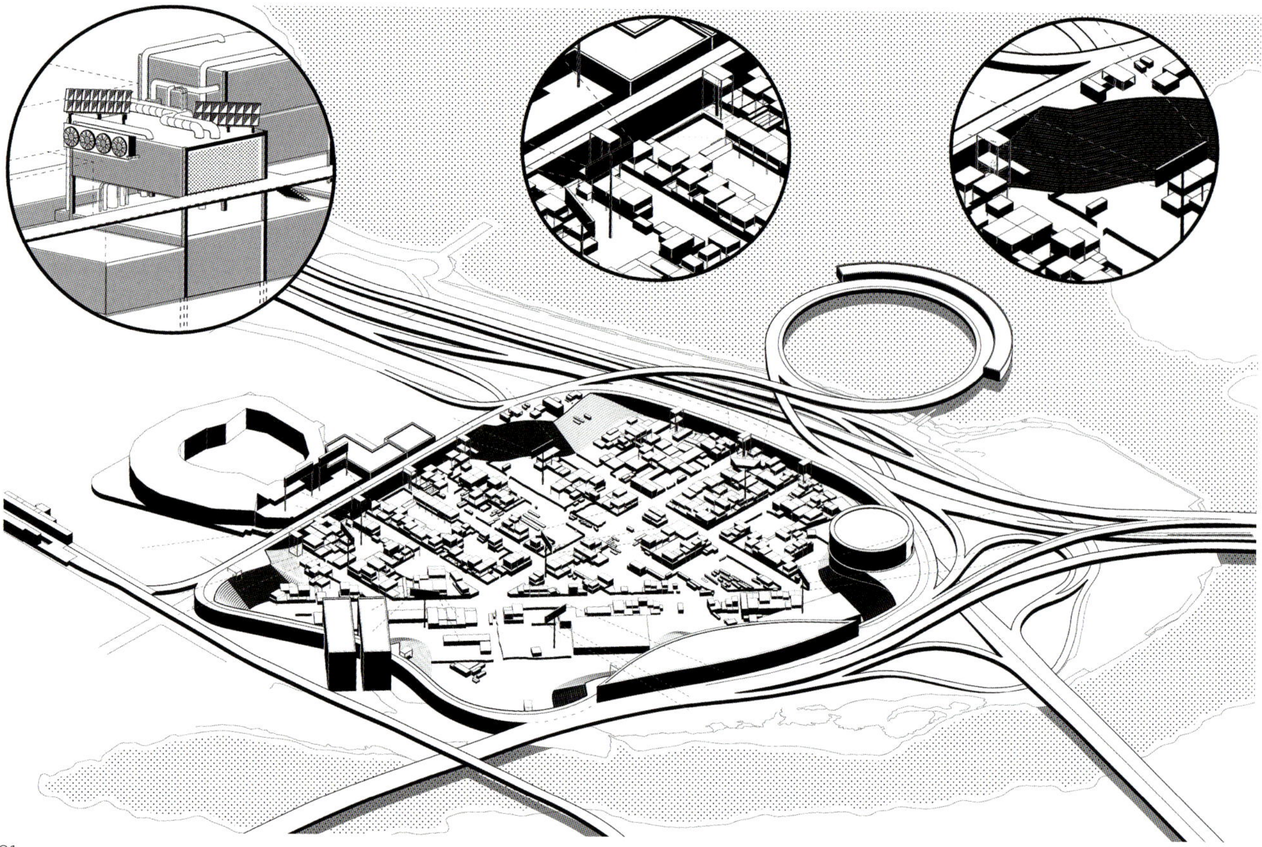

01

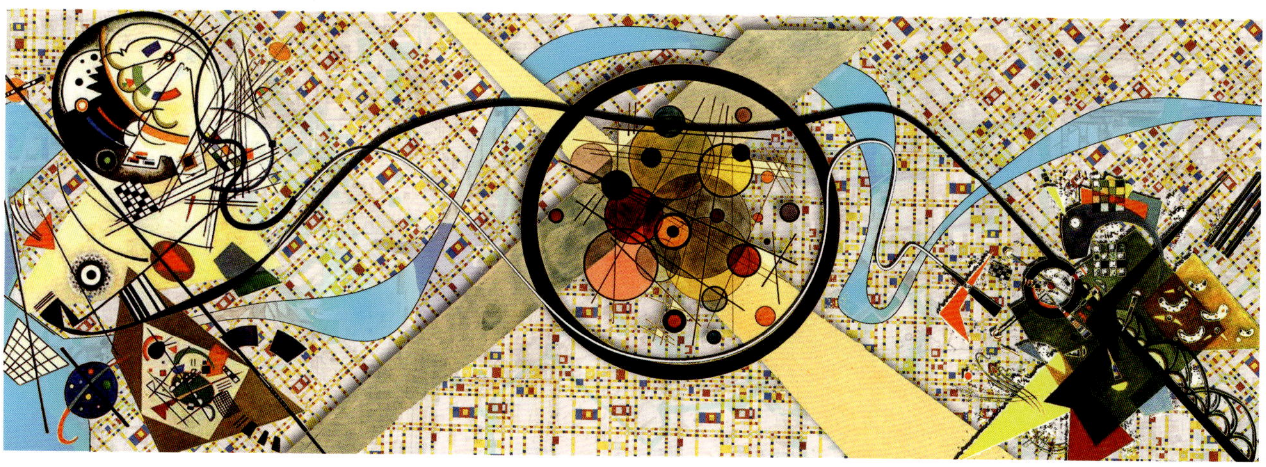

02

03

04

01-03 | David Lee
04 | David McConnell

IN-SITU URBANIZTION

The exponential development of urban centers due to the rural migration does not affect city centers alone. Urbanity, as well as industry, infrastructures and global investment, circulates form the urban centers back into the rural periphery. Against the familiar top-down formalist design that shapes city centers, the 'unplanned' unban fringe is emerging; constantly shaped by multiplicity of global and local agencies without the coordination of regional authorities.

In- Situ examines the potential of urban transformations in the city fringe to prospect an alternative to the projected urbanism of the global city. It considers the existing rural fabric as an infrastructural and social scaffold for process of modernization and spatial change. Within this frame work, it addresses the current challenges of an urbanized world; Secured food distribution, balanced energy consumption, Sustainable social arrangements and preservation of the natural environments.

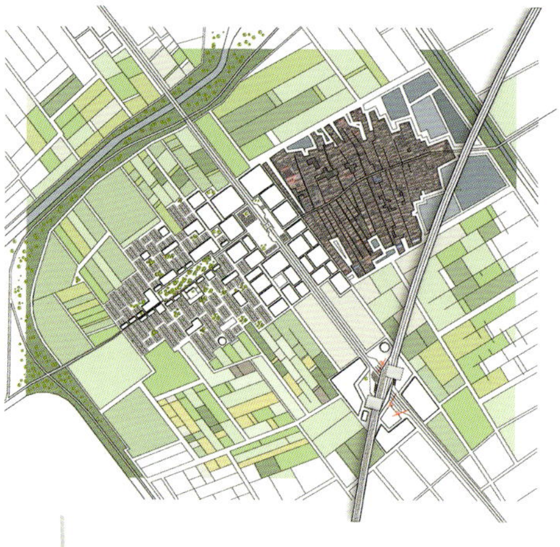

01

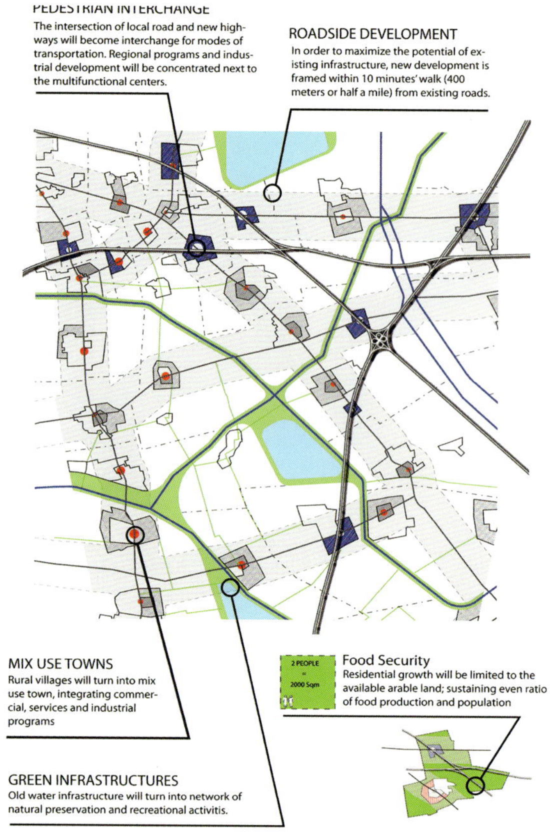

02

03

04

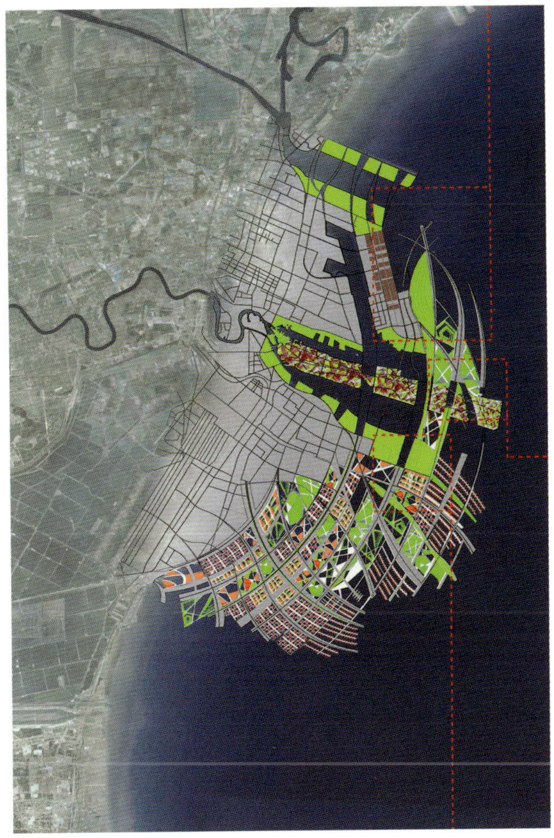

05

06

01, 02 | Ofer Bilik
03 | Carlos Rodriguez
04 | Blake Fortson
05, 06 | Adra Bubesi

MAST

OF LANDSCAPE ARCHITECTURE

ER

1st SEMESTER DESIGN

FACULTY
Catherine Seavitt-Nordenson / Mersiha Veledar

"The time will come when New York will be built up... and the picturesquely varied, rocky formations of the island will have been converted into formations for rows of monotonous straight streets, and piles of erect buildings. There will be no suggestion left of its present varied surfaces, with the single exception of the few acres contained in the Park."
– Frederick Law Olmsted

This is an introductory studio in landscape architectural design, studying the origins and conventions of drawing and representation in landscape architecture. Spatial relationships, and the abstract qualities of space itself, are examined using photography, measurement and description, two-dimensional projections, and three-dimensional models.

Emphasis is placed on the use of the section as a tool for studying the establishment of a horizontal datum, the development of vertical organization, the volumetric displacement of earth, and the abstracted description of terrain. Analytic mapping of systemic site conditions is also explored, as well as a programmatically developed design intervention. Olmsted's North Woods in Central Park is the source for both the exploration of representational and analytic techniques and a design proposal. Traversed by a deep ravine, this 90-acre hardwood forest within the park was imagined by Olmsted as a simulacrum of the Adirondack Mountains, a grafting of sublime wild nature into the city. The surrounding city disappears upon entering the Loch and Ravine; the North Woods is an extraordinary example of the American picturesque embedded within an urban context.

Catherine Seavitt-Nordenson
Studio 1 Landscape Design

Sara Malmkvist
CATHERINE SEAVITT-NORDENSON, CRITIC

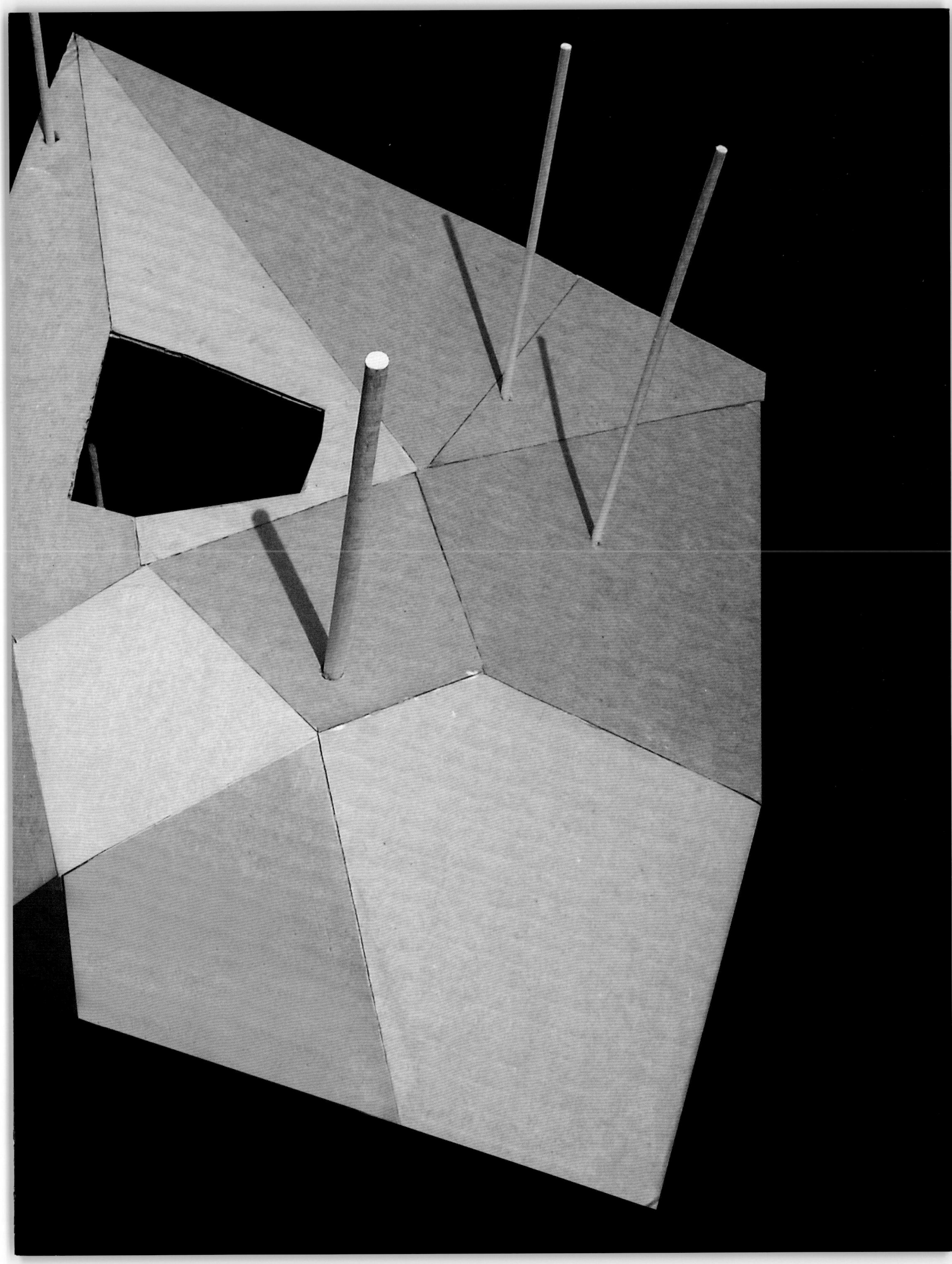

01

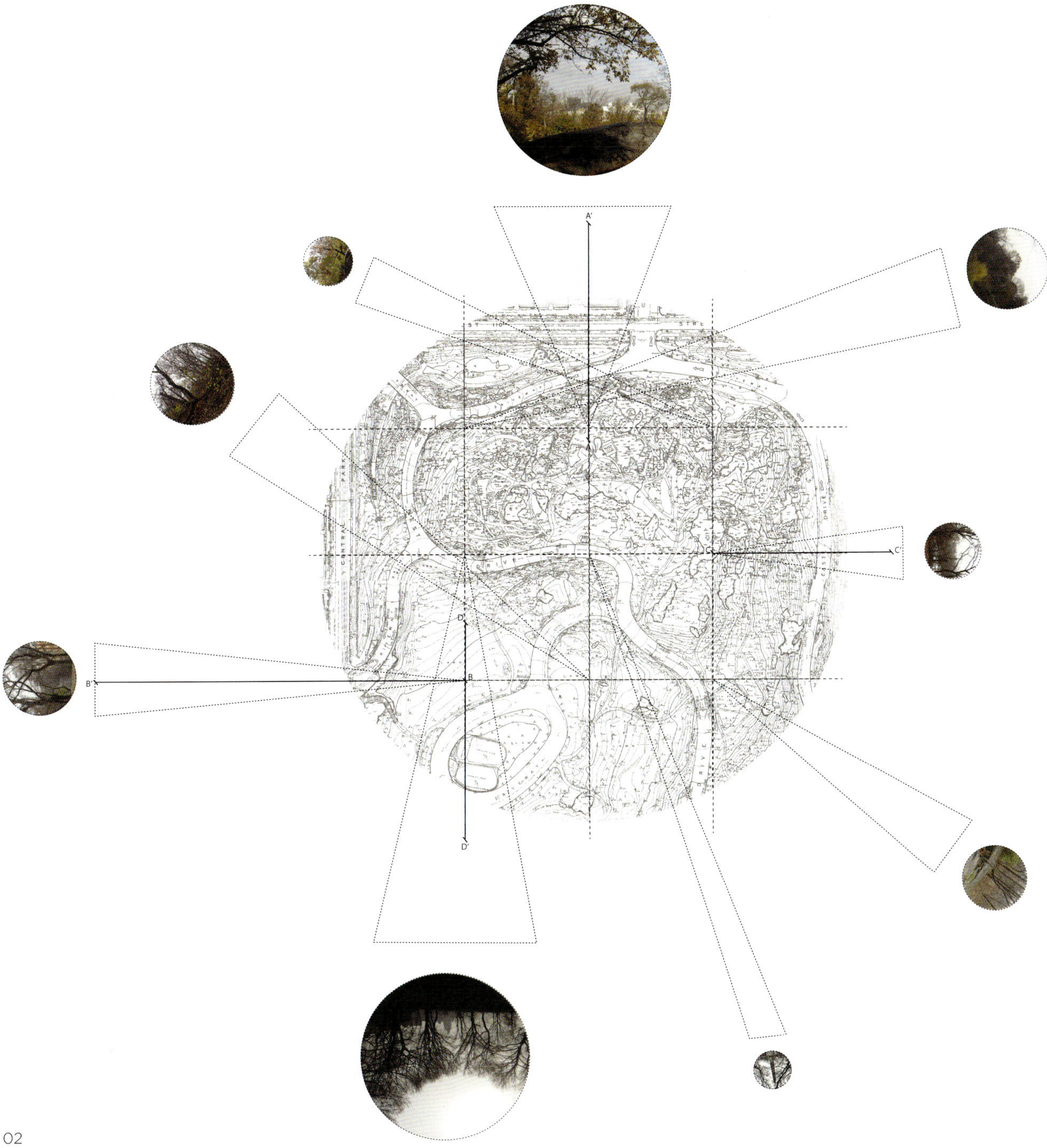

02

01 | Eli Sands
02 | Kirsten Myhr

2nd SEMESTER DESIGN

FACULTY
Denise Hoffman-Brandt / Andrew Zientek / Isaac Gertman

Waterproofing New York

With two destructive tropical storms in two years, New York City—like other global cities—is entering a phase of adaptation to catastrophic climate events which are a result of carbon cycle disruption by human, urban and industrial practices. Superstorm recovery will require more than a simple fix; it will necessitate systemic adaptation to escalating storm surge, precipitation, and wind events through the construction of new urban landscapes that have the capacity to merge social, cultural, and environmental forces. This studio will explore planning strategies and design tactics for that new "waterproofed" urban landscapes. The studio was initiated with an investigation of New York City's infrastructural sectors that was supported by the Waterproofing New York conference at the SSA on February 9, 2013. Of course, classifying the sectors for the event revealed overlap across systems. For example, Fuel is Power and Fuel is critical to Circulation. Shelter is dependent on Water, Waste and Power. Fluidity in the classification was deemed beneficial as it provoked cross-sector strategic thinking.

Denise Hoffman-Brandt
Director, Master of Landscape Architecture Program

Jerome Thomson
ANDREW ZIENTEK/ ISAAC GERTMAN, CRITICS

POWER IN A NEW LIGHT

FORGING RELATIONSHIPS WITH COMMUNITY, INFRASTRUCTURE, AND NOCTURNAL LANDSCAPES

A GLIMPSE OF OUR CURRENT ENERGY NETWORK AND ITS IMPACT ON RED HOOK HOUSES

Households Affected by Power Outages During Superstorm Sandy

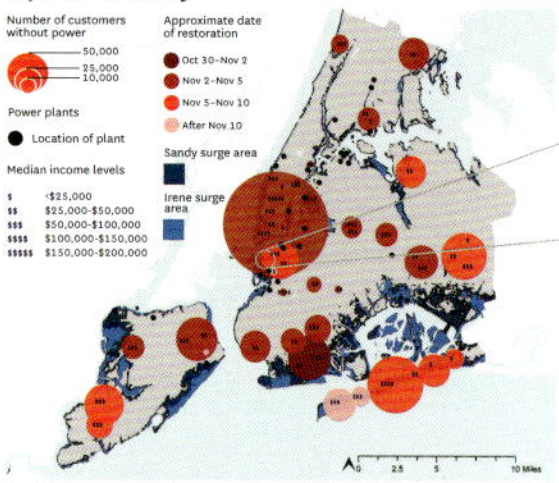

Sources: Con Edison, Wednesday 10/31/2012 12 pm, Long Island Power Authority for the Rockaways

Red Hook Houses and Superstorm Sandy

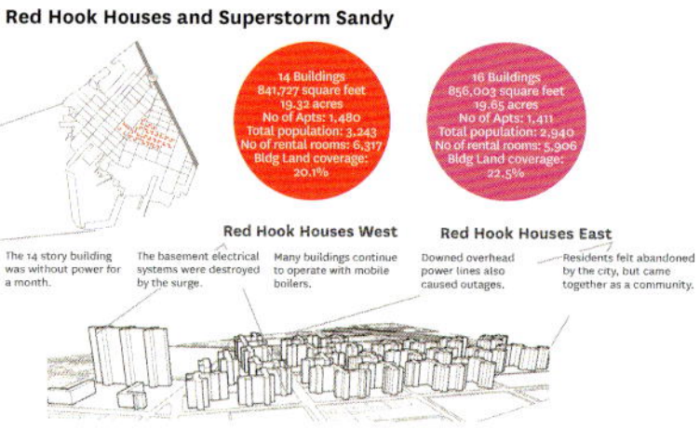

New York's Peak Demand

Peak demand, periods of strong consumer demand, fluctuating daily, monthly, or seasonally can exceed the maximum supply levels that the electrical power industry can generate, resulting in power outages and load shedding.

Energy Lost in Production & Transmission

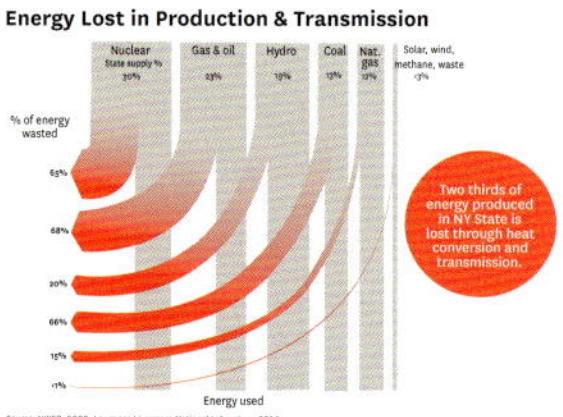

Source: NYISO, 2009, Lawrence Livermore National Laboratory, 2011.

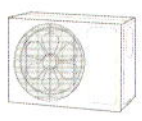

There are 6.3 million window AC units in NYC, with another million expected over the next five years. When millions of the ACs are operating at the same time during hot summer days, they consume about one-fifth of the city's peak load.

New York's Energy Network

The current power grid is composed of many vulnerable parts, and each piece must be working correctly for the end user to receive electricity.

- Petroleum terminal
- Electric facility
- Gas facility
- Wind farm
- Nuclear plant
- Electric transmission line
- Gas transmission line

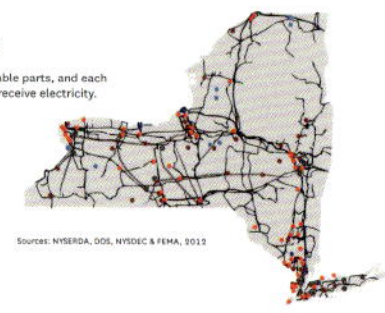

Sources: NYSERDA, DOS, NYSDEC & FEMA, 2012

EXPOSING INVISIBILITIES AND RETHINKING INFRASTRUCTURE SITING

Red Hook Houses' infrastructure of solidarity was more more resilient than its physical infrastructure, which left some residents without power for more than a month. With climate change we will need to adjust our thinking of the way we site physical infrastructure. It needs to become more robust and redundant, but should also integrate into the landscape in a more nuanced, scalable fashion.

Red Hook Houses' Solar Capacity

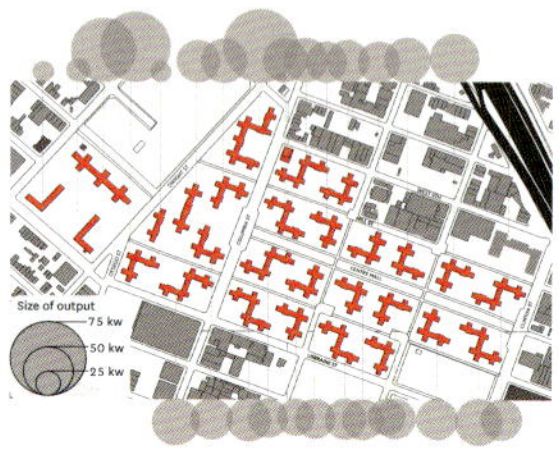

Annual Power Consumption

Electricity use: 12,002 mWh
Total fuel use: 2,071,475 Therms
Land area: 1,792,406 square feet

Estimated Annual Energy End Use Split %

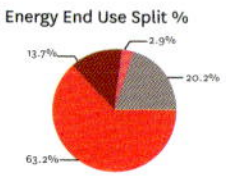

Data Source: Spatial distribution of urban building energy consumption http://modi.mech.columbia.edu/nycenergy/

Potential Production

The 30 RHHs could produce a combined 2,365.2 Mwh of energy annually. That would account for 20% of their current energy consumption.

Energy and Economy Over Time

The Jevon's Paradox- "Technological progress that increases the efficiency with which a resource is used, tends to increase (rather than decrease) the rate of consumption of that resource." -William Stanley Jevon's, The Coal Question, 1865.

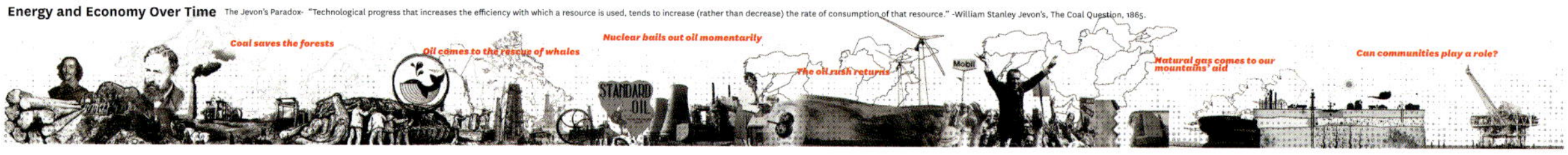

01

ILLUMINATING AND LINKING COMMUNITY

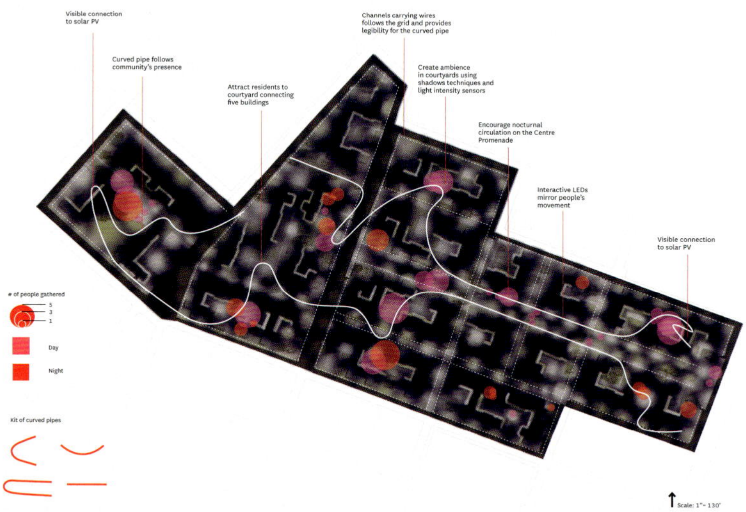

BEFORE

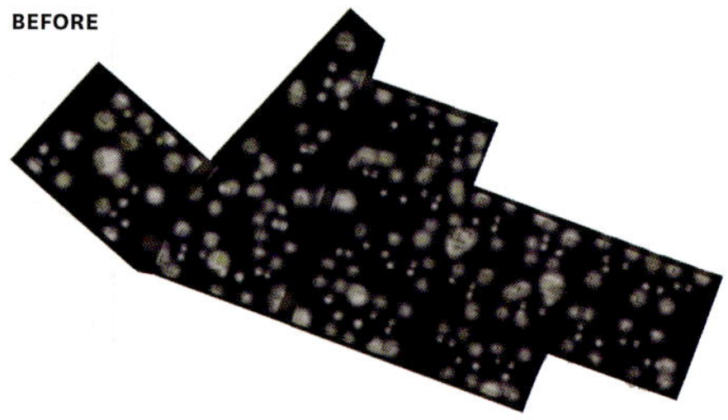

AFTER

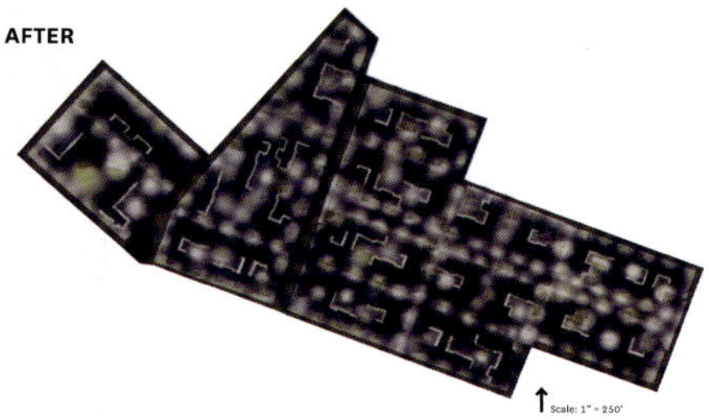

LIGHTING STRATEGIES

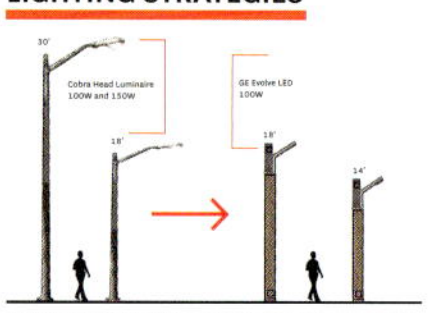

The lights will be lowered in height to humanize scale, and to allow for a more consistent non uniform spread.

Re-scale

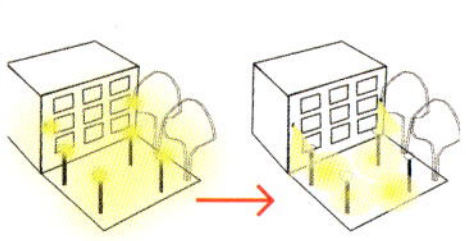

High Pressure Sodium Lamps emit light in all directions while LEDs emit light in a specific direction. This reduces the need for reflectors and diffusers, resulting in less wasted light and more efficiency.

Shift to useful light

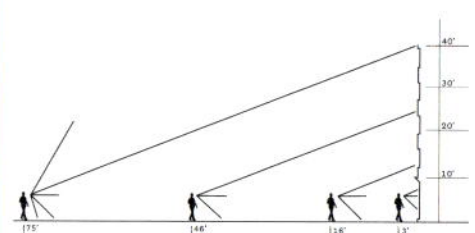

There is no need to illuminate the upper floors of building facades for security reasons as pedestrians can see less than 10 feet of the building when they are close to the building. Source: Close Encounters

Remove light from building facades

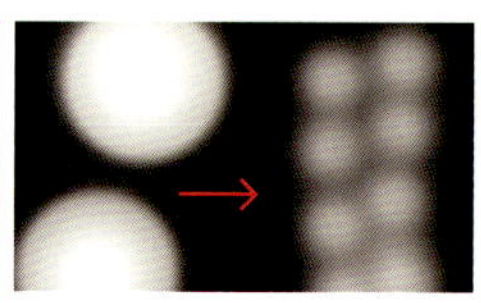

Uniform lighting produces glare. The wider placement of uniform luminaires requires repeated eye readjustment and creates eyestrain and temporary blindness when entering and leaving light pools.

Create non-uniform spread

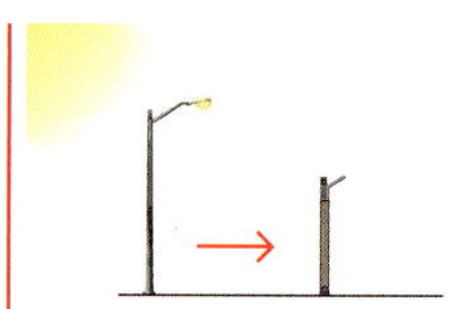

The lights at Red Hook Houses are currently powered 24 hours a day.

Power off during the day

02

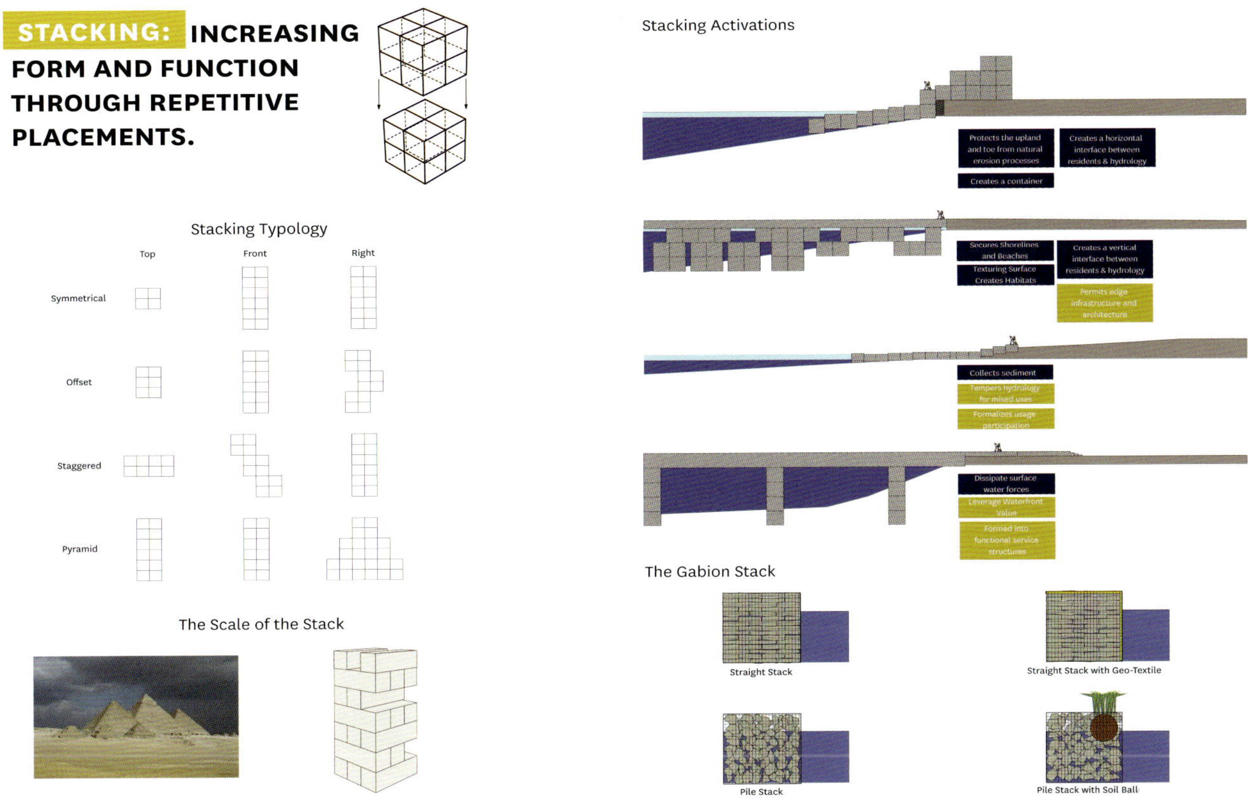

03

04

01, 02 | Andrea Johnson
03, 04 | Eli Sands

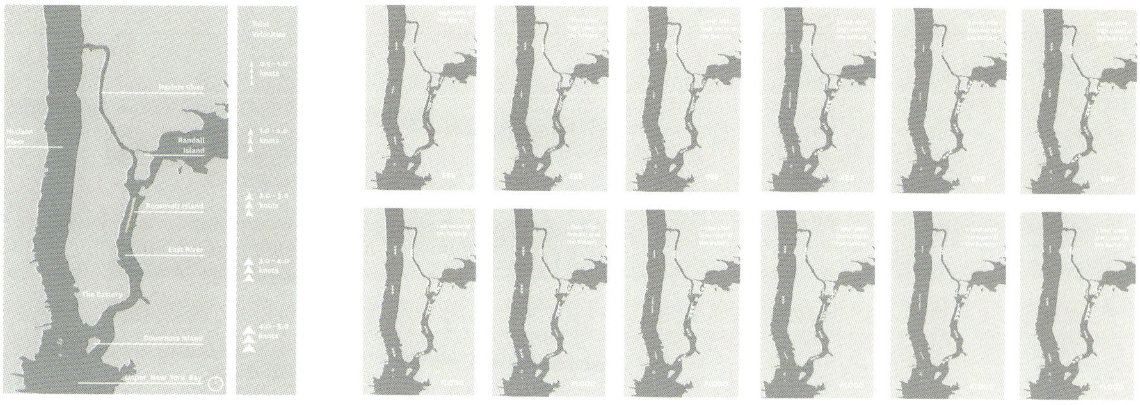

01

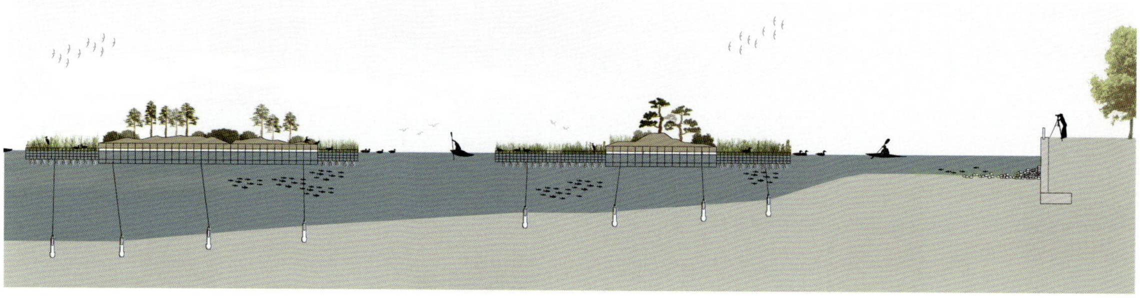

02

THE THREE MODULES

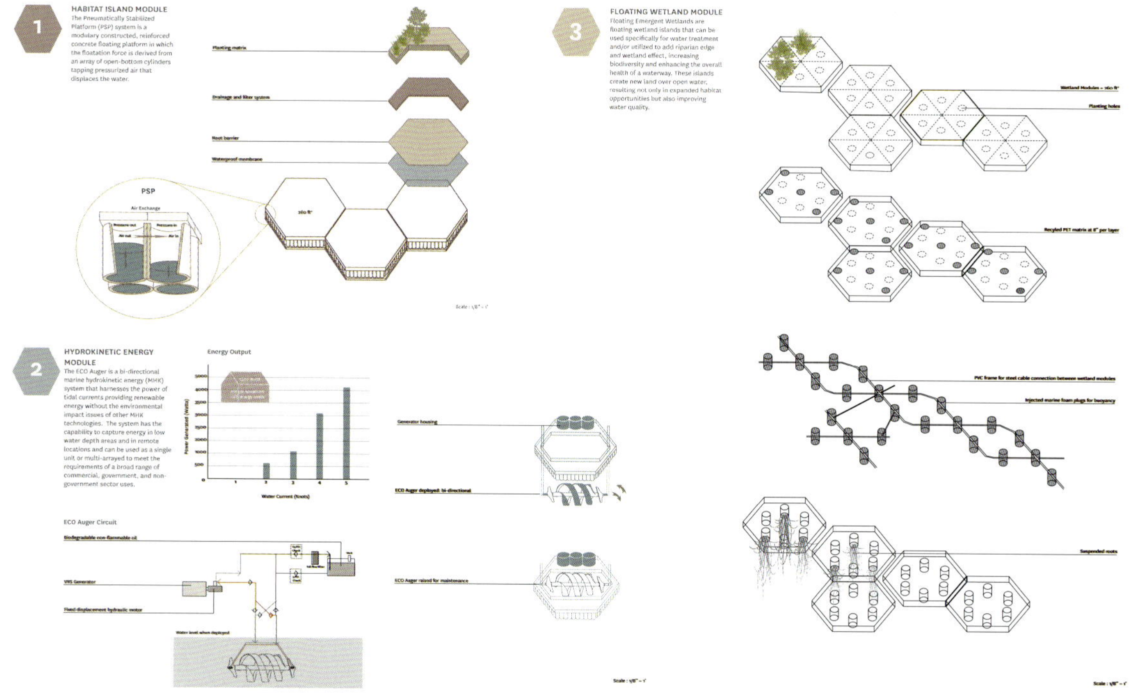

03

ANATOMICALLY INCORRECT: BELLEVUE & NYU LANGONE HOSPTALS

Our East side hospitals are in a flood zone and need to be protected from storm surge. Building a sea wall remedies storm surge from the river but does not account for run off from higher avenues; a bathtub affect. I propose to raise the FDR and fortify the hospitals and surrounding streets with walls and elevated ramps.

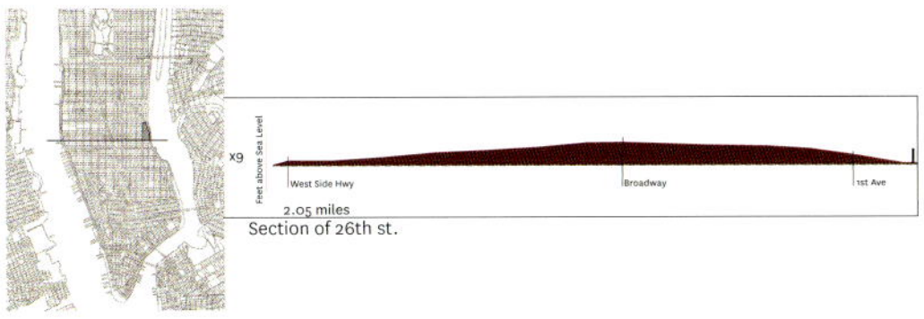

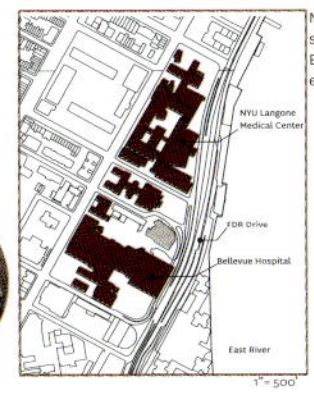

NYU & Bellevue are separated from the East River by the FDR, elevation 3'

The 14' surge poured over the FDR flooding both hospitals causing power outages, evacuations and long term infrastructural & educational damage.

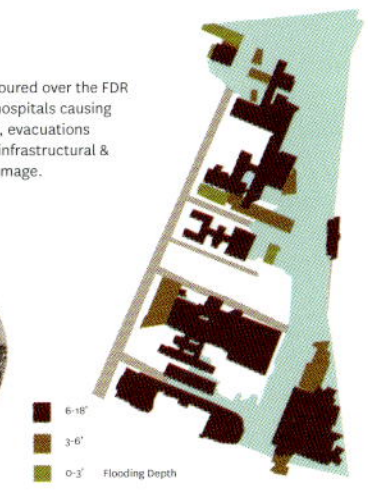

Phase 1

Prepare for hospital fortification

Hierarchy of Cuts

Relocate non-critical care and ambulatory surgery to other locations within city

Utilize other NYU clinic facility locations

Relocate Emergency rooms to higher, safer floors

Communicate new locations with universal medical codes

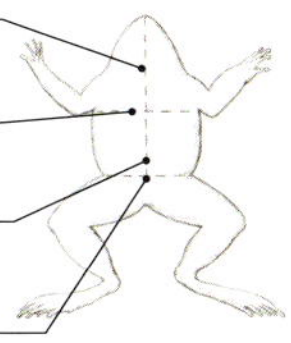

Dissect the Hospitals

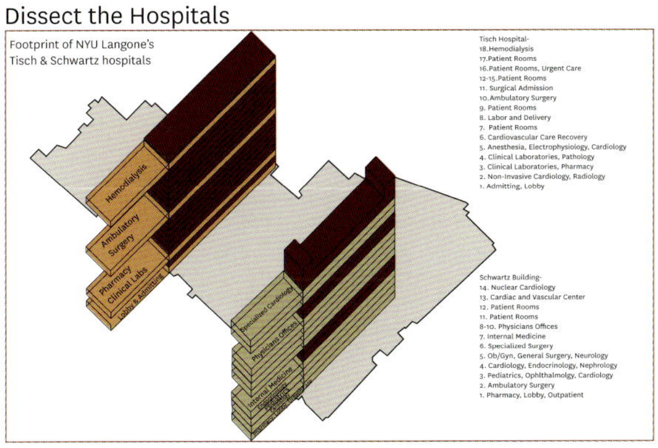

A. Establish which floors hold critical care/emergency facilities, ambulatory clinics and offices.

B. Differentiate between critical care, ambulatory clinics and offices to determine site specificity.

C. Redistribute non-critical care

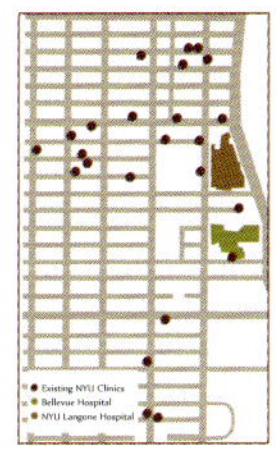

Identify issues with insurance plans to encourage use of satellite clinics.

"ACUTE CARE RESOURCES ARE SCARCE FOR THE UNINSURED AND UNDER-INSURED" -St. Louis Urgent Care

04

Repurpose structures for multi-functionality

Multi-functional characteristics of the newly elevated FDR will benefit the neighborhood by providing space for a new park, new pedestrian and bicycle lanes, bioswales and parking. Proposed ramps will provide direct access to newly raised emergency rooms. Vacant first 3 hospital floors will be repurposed for rain water collection cisterns.

Multi-level functionality is integral in an urban landscape.

Utilizing the FDR for parking allows for new plant and soil communities on the coast and in the streets.

Geocells assist in establishing plant and soil communities in difficult areas.

Soil assists in absorption and provides a stable medium for plants.

Plant communities stabilize new coastal environments.

C. Repurpose under-utilized coastal area as a terraced park; Re-introduce plant and soil communities to a sealed surface and expand running paths to offer multi level experience.

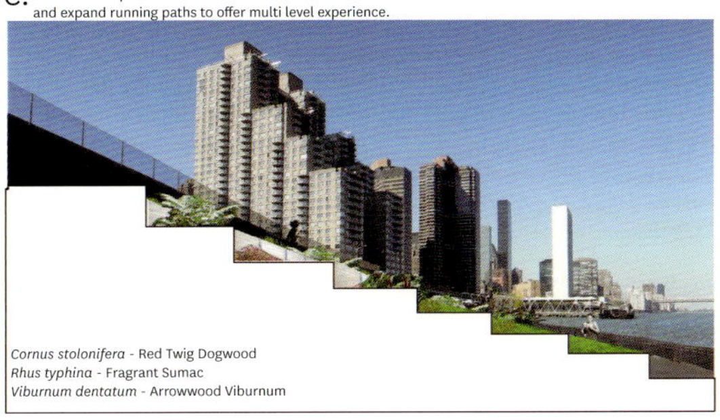

D. Introducing new parking beneath the FDR allows street parking to be transferred which provides an extra lane for bicycles and bioswales.

A pedestrian bridge provides access from 34th St. to the new terraced park

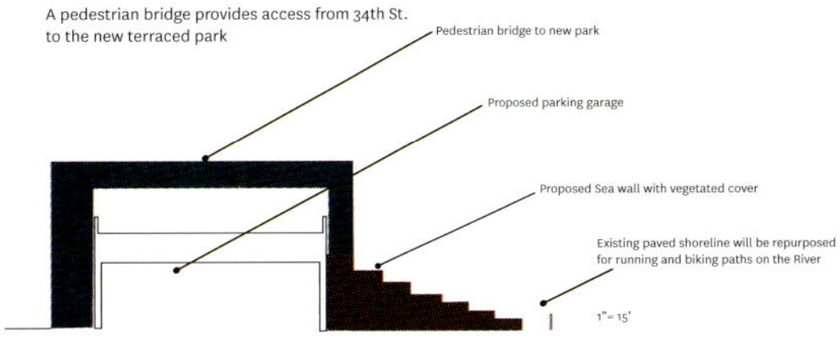

05

01-03 | Fern Lan Siew
04, 05 | Julia Millea

3rd SEMESTER DESIGN

FACULTY
Lee Weintraub / Barbara Wilks

ENTANGLEMENTS
Finding form to make a place from the various forces working on a site

Now that the studio has, in previous studio sequences, learned the basic skills of landscape architecture, the Third Semester Design studio concentrates on combining those basic learned skills of landscape architecture with observation, analysis, perception and value systems to create places and platforms which connect human interaction and environmental processes.

The students are asked to apply observation and critical thinking to create program rich environments that add value to a community through design. In an evolving and rapidly changing urban context of environment and community, the studio will develop a process of investigation and design which results in a series of projects that can be tested for both their fit and connection, as well as for their transformative effect. The studio will complete two different comprehensive project investigations this semester—the first quickly to develop our process, and the second with more time to refine and develop the design. Both projects will be taken to design development, a final stage of the formal design process. For this studio's investigation, design development means not only having a concept which brings together the various strands of the project, but also through more substantial detail, defines the character of the place and creates relationships between the various forces working on the site—and entangles them to make a place.

The projects include a stair in topographically challenging upper Manhattan, and a waterfront site within the Brooklyn Navy Yard that has been recently inundated by the surge of the East River during Sandy.

Lee Weintraub
Studio II Landscape Design

Sam Berkheiser
LEE WEINTRAUB, CRITIC

01

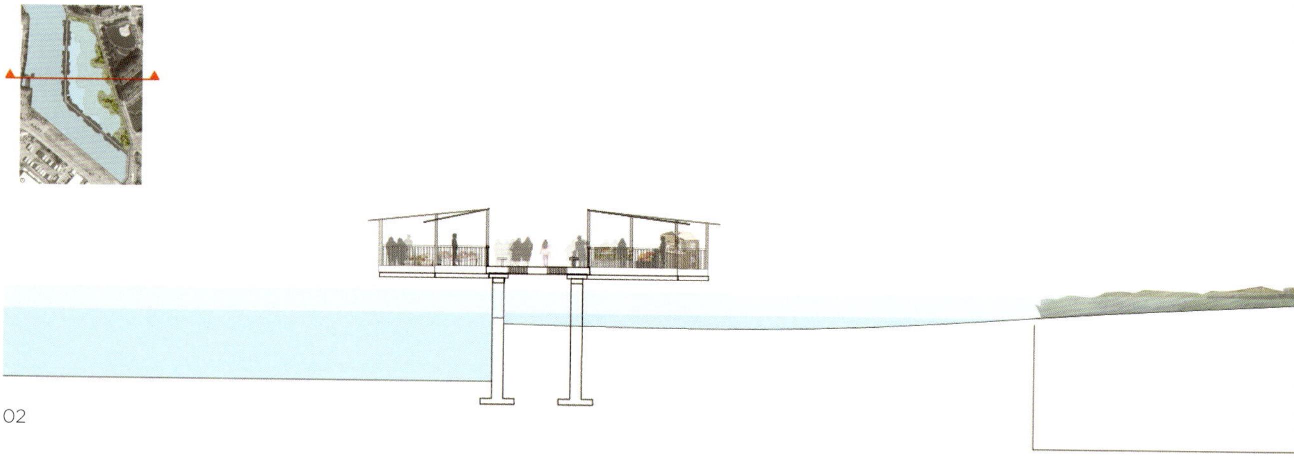

02

03

01 | Sam Berkheiser
02, 03 | Lara Gelband

01

02

03

04

05

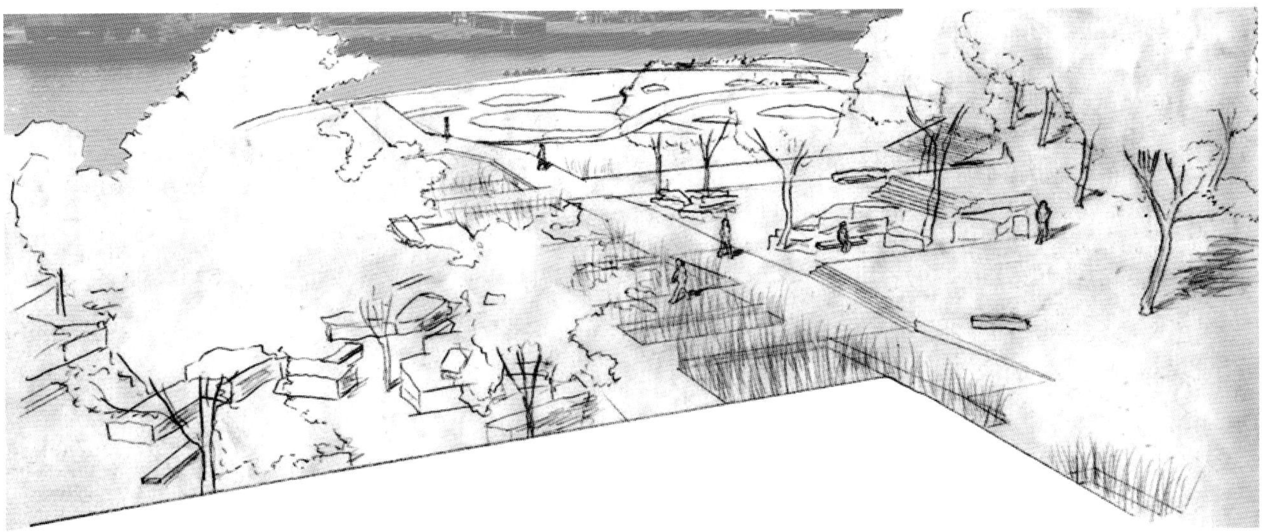

06

01-05 | David Mosey
06 | Ryan Morrison

4th SEMESTER DESIGN

FACULTY
Peter Gisolfi / Lee Weintraub

Undertaken by both the landscape and architecture students, the Elizabeth study should be placed in a larger regional lens that "follows the water" from its upland origins through the downtown, as well as the impact of tidal backflows and surges from the Arthur Kill. Teams should discuss the technical challenges of building in areas that may be subject to future flooding, and should map these areas from the outset of the studio. How do we generate designs that mine the full potential of the often dormant or subsumed traits of natural systems and of urban systems that serves Elizabeth and contribute mightily to it's growth and prosperity. While the emphasis of the architecture studio is focused on development of approaches and solutions to shelter, the study area also presents opportunities for other kinds of building and landscape typologies. These support the place and purpose of Elizabeth and, as the collaborative teams explore and discuss solutions will present a further opportunity for both incremental and transformative change.

Peter Gisolfi
Second Year Landscape Design Coordinator

Ryan Morrison
LEE WEINTRAUB , CRITIC

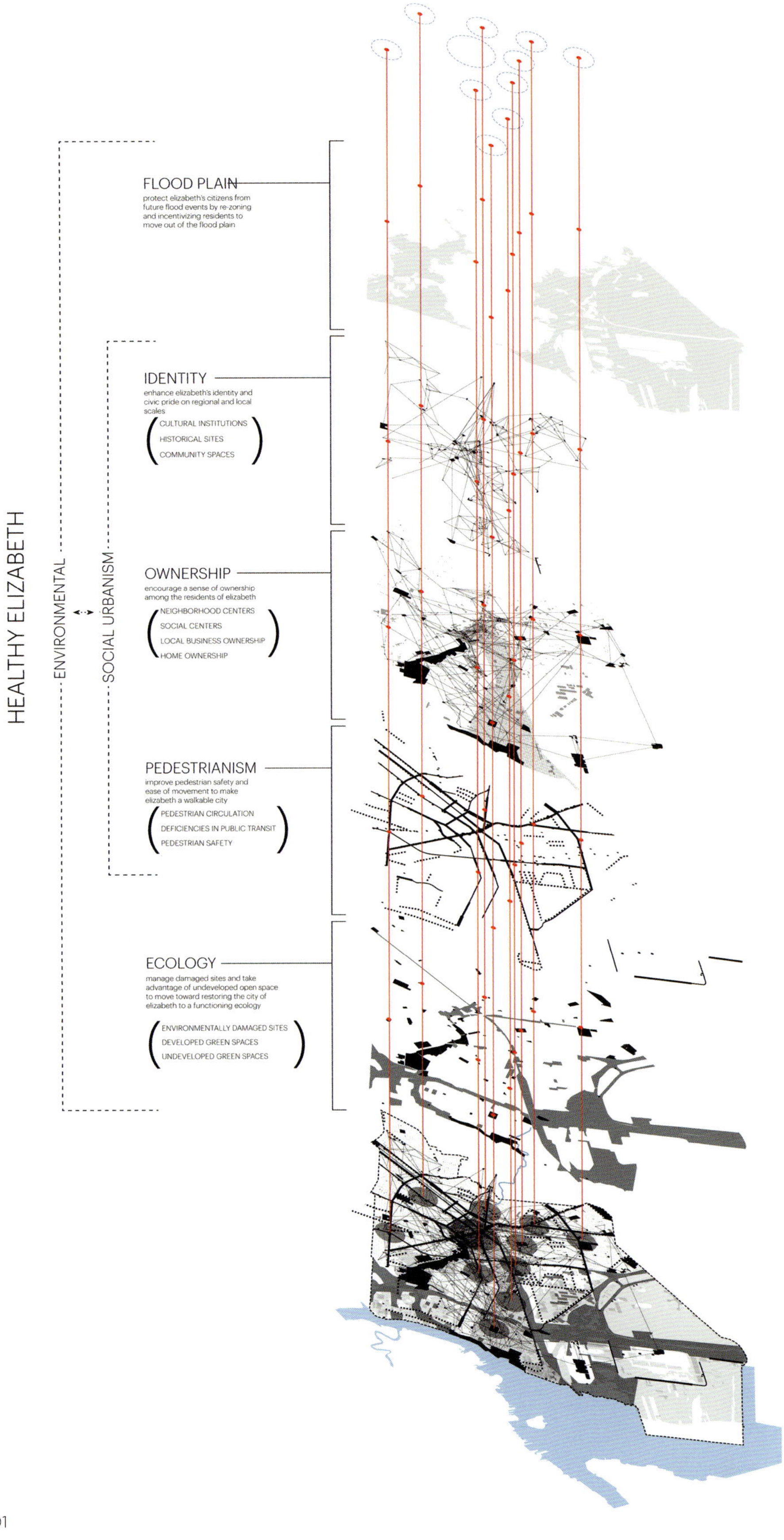
HEALTHY ELIZABETH
ENVIRONMENTAL
SOCIAL URBANISM
FLOOD PLAIN
protect elizabeth's citizens from future flood events by re-zoning and incentivizing residents to move out of the flood plain
IDENTITY
enhance elizabeth's identity and civic pride on regional and local scales
CULTURAL INSTITUTIONS
HISTORICAL SITES
COMMUNITY SPACES
OWNERSHIP
encourage a sense of ownership among the residents of elizabeth
NEIGHBORHOOD CENTERS
SOCIAL CENTERS
LOCAL BUSINESS OWNERSHIP
HOME OWNERSHIP
PEDESTRIANISM
improve pedestrian safety and ease of movement to make elizabeth a walkable city
PEDESTRIAN CIRCULATION
DEFICIENCIES IN PUBLIC TRANSIT
PEDESTRIAN SAFETY
ECOLOGY
manage damaged sites and take advantage of undeveloped open space to move toward restoring the city of elizabeth to a functioning ecology
ENVIRONMENTALLY DAMAGED SITES
DEVELOPED GREEN SPACES
UNDEVELOPED GREEN SPACES

01

02

03

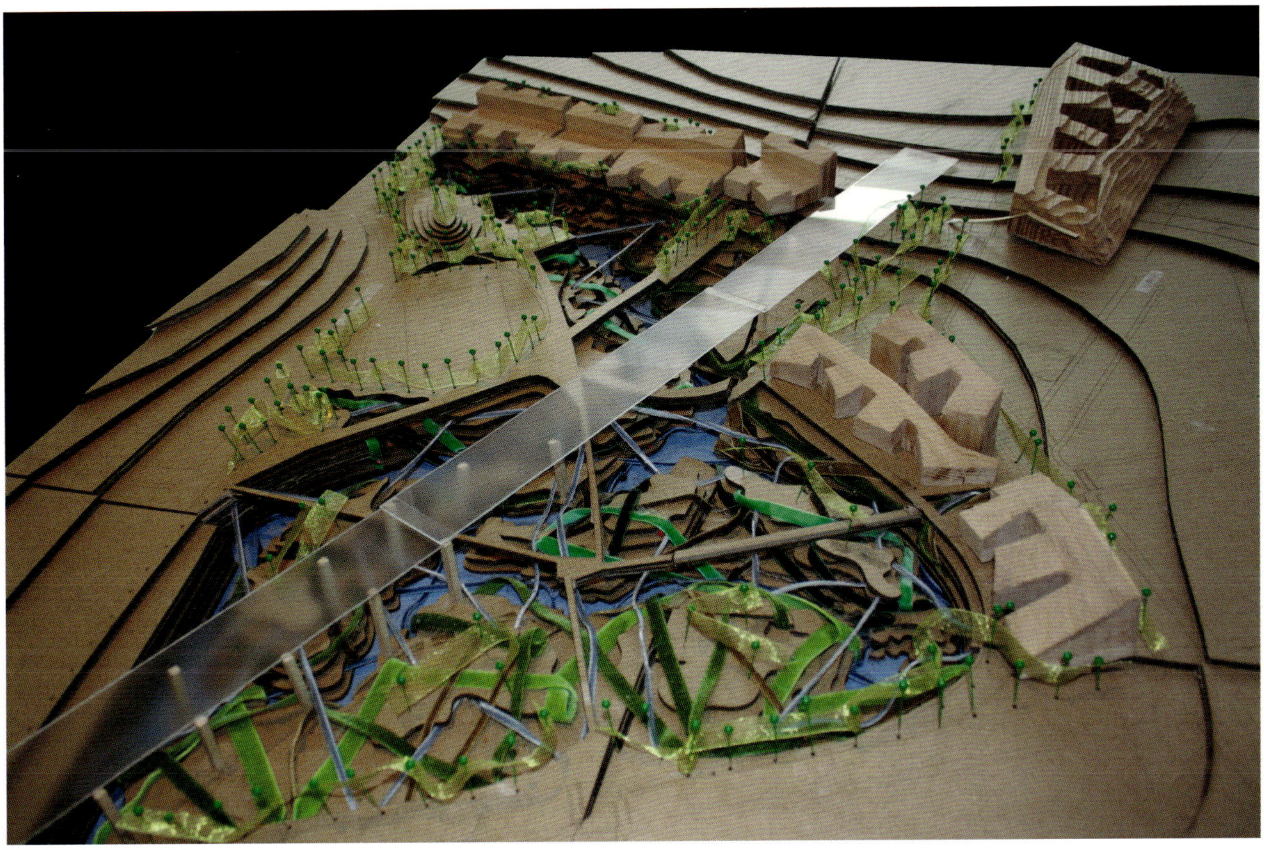

04

01 | Ryan Morrison
02-04 | Grace Ng

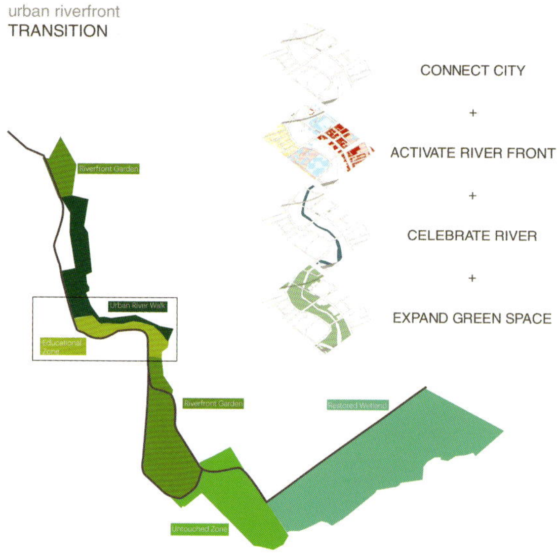
urban riverfront
TRANSITION
CONNECT CITY
+
ACTIVATE RIVER FRONT
+
CELEBRATE RIVER
+
EXPAND GREEN SPACE
Riverfront Garden
Urban River Walk
Educational Zone
Riverfront Garden
Restored Wetland
Untouched Zone

01

02

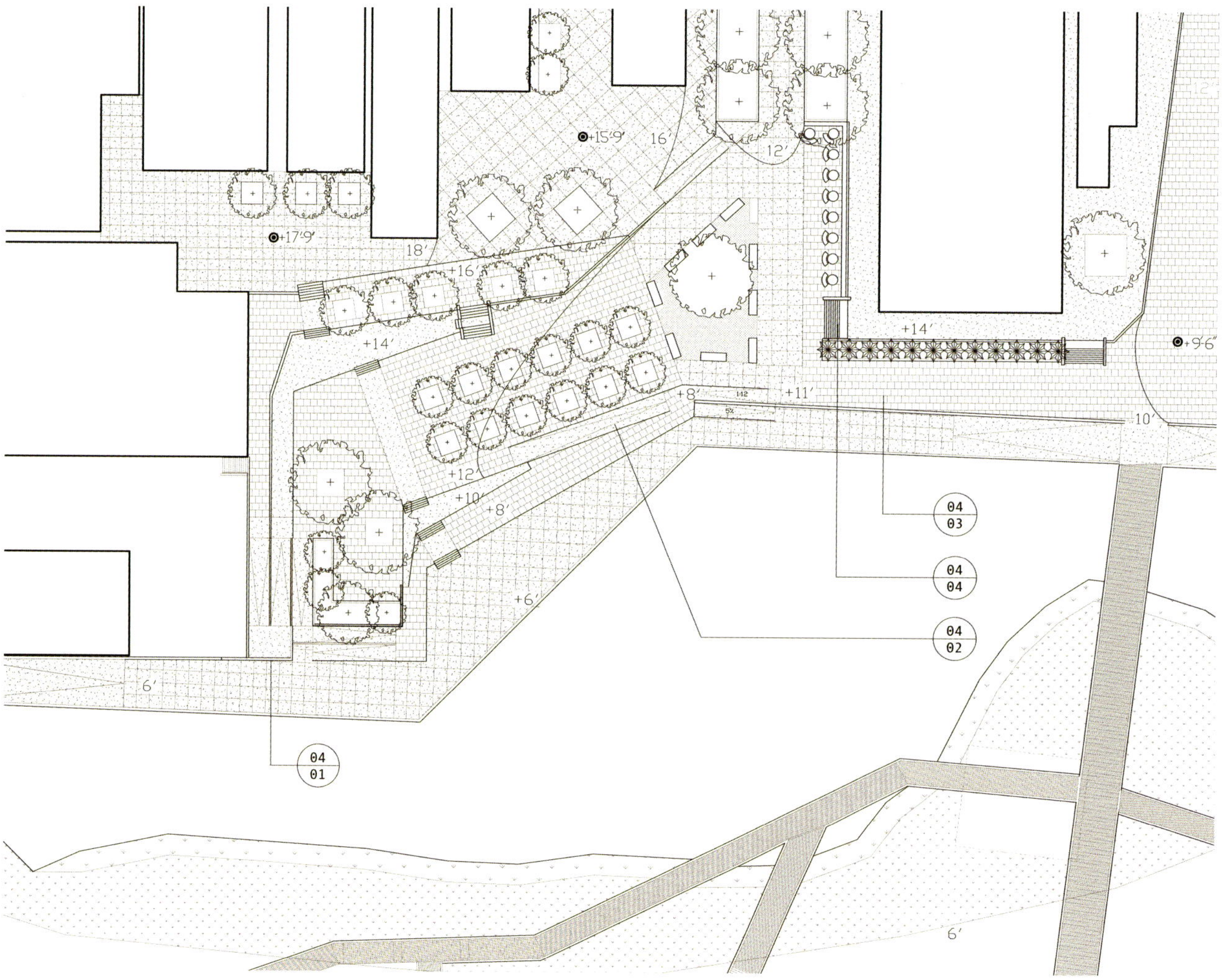
+15'9"
16'
12'
+17'9"
18'
+16
+14'
+14'
+9'6"
+8'
+11'
10'
+12
+10
+8'
+6'
6'
6'
04
03
04
04
04
02
04
01

03

04

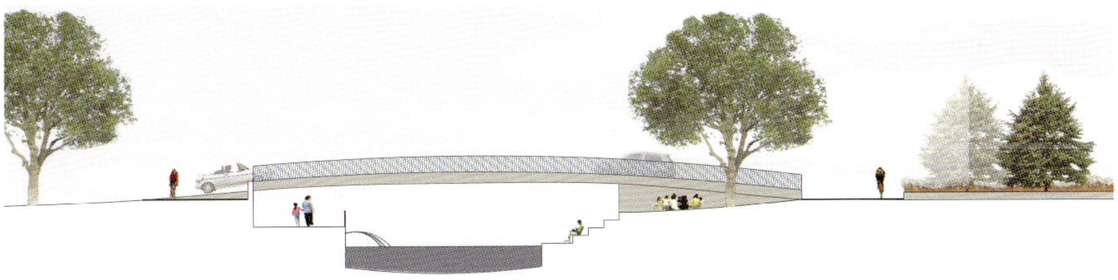

05

06

01-03 | Adam Thyberg
04-06 | Daniel Turgeon

5th SEMESTER DESIGN

FACULTY
Denise Hoffman-Brandt / Brett Seamans

City H2O

Cities are ecological systems; they are the collective anthropogenic and environmental system processes sustaining the human organism.

There is a strong tradition of assessing the degrading affects of urbanism's environmental impacts; but the phenomenal changes that cities will undergo as they adapt, or not, to climate change, are only now beginning to enter the discourse of urban landscape architecture. This is likely due to the fifty-year long, and ongoing, debate over the credibility of climate science that forecasts "global warming" and the difficulty the public has in relating that raging debate to its daily lives. For citizens the idea of climate change and the awareness of its potential impacts on their perceivable world are not synthetic.

In the City H2O studio, students explored the processes and phenomena associated with climate change in two explicit urban environments that face extremes of difference in how they will be affected by forecasted climate change: Phoenix and New York City. Each student developed design proposals intended to define their position on urban water issues, and sought to provoke public engagement in a colloquy through their inhabitation of the proposed landscapes.

Denise Hoffman-Brandt
Director, Master of Landscape Architecture Program

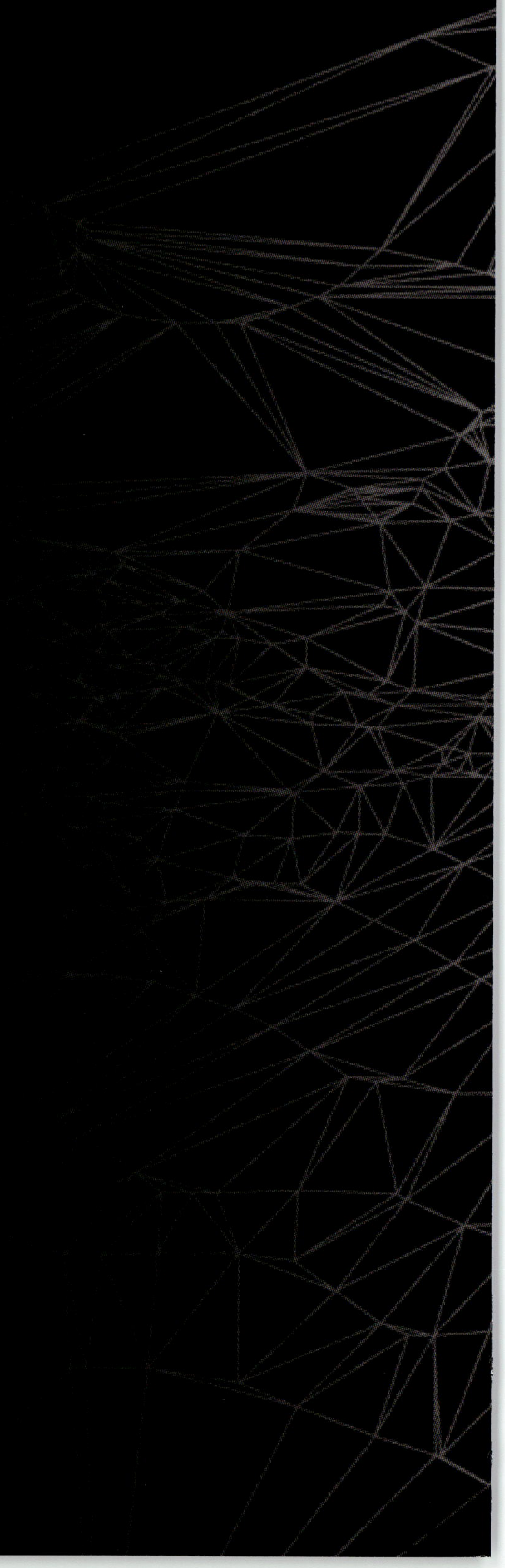

Jihong Kim
DENISE HOFFMAN-BRANDT / BRETT SEAMANS, CRITICS

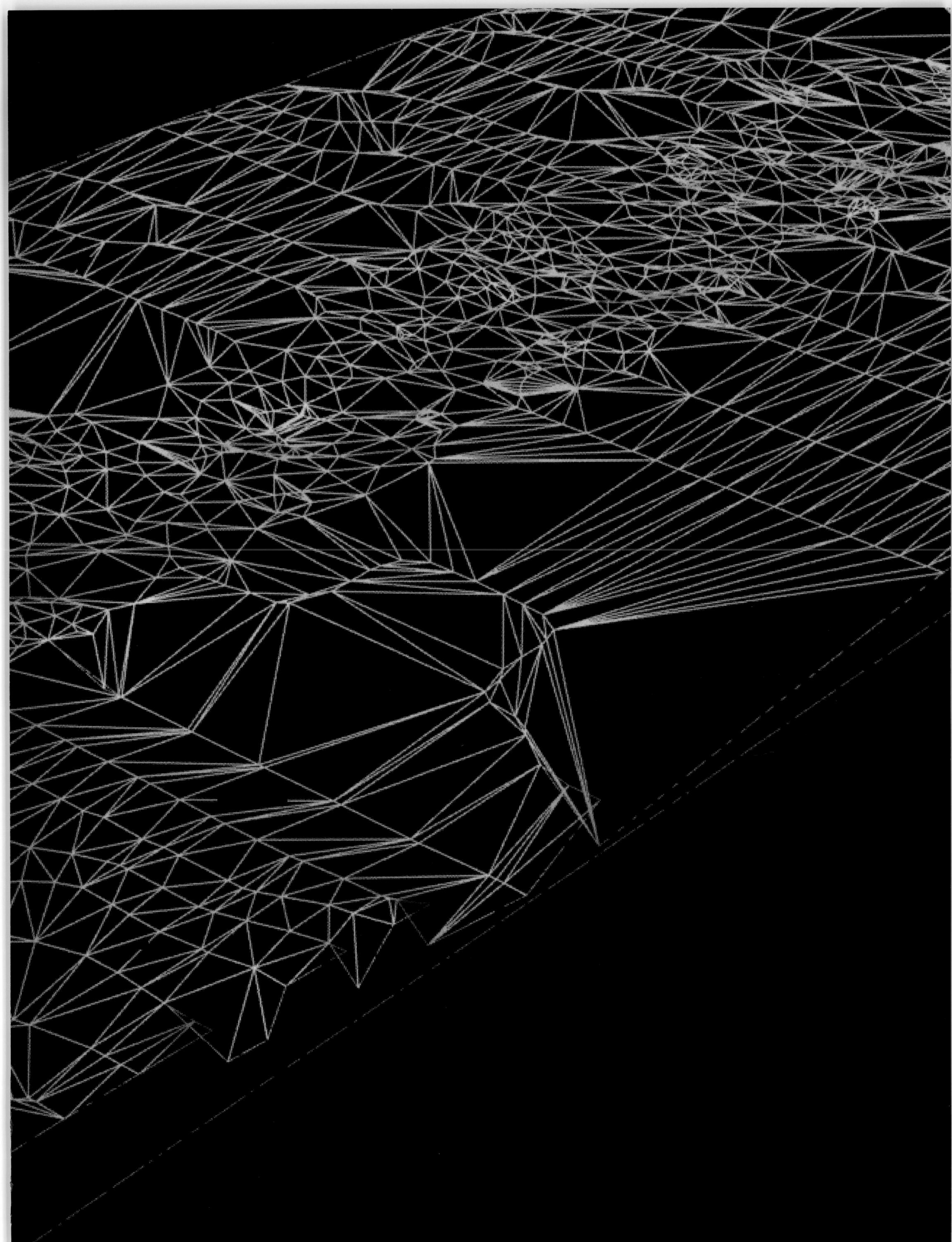

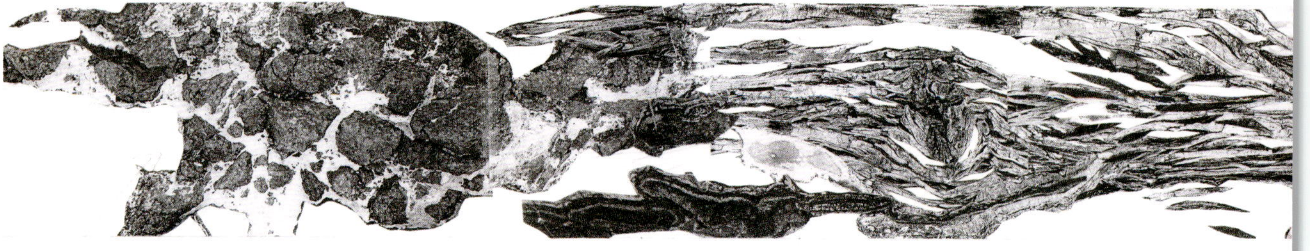

01

02

03

04

05

06

07

08

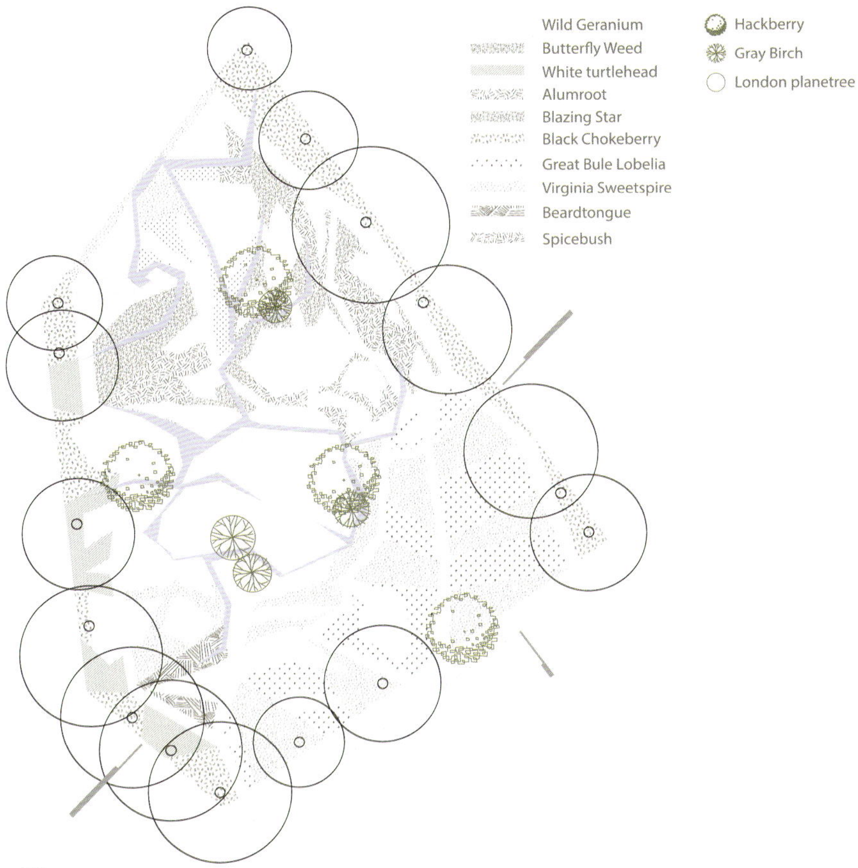

09

01 | Sheila Moss
02-08 | Pavlo Sotiriou
09 | Jihong Kim

6th SEMESTER THESIS

FACULTY
Catherine Seavitt-Nordenson / Scott Shell

The Comprehensive Design Studio is the last in the sequence of six landscape architecture design studios, and the culmination of the Master of Landscape Architecture program's design sequence. Students in the Comprehensive Design Studio work independently under the supervision of two faculty advisors. This independent studio follows the development of an original thesis topic developed in the Fall 2012 Design Research seminar.

The work developed in the studio addresses a clearly defined contemporary problem seen through the lens of the discipline of landscape architecture. Each student's work is developed as a series of design research probes, each operating within the field of landscape architecture. Research and design development within any site thus considers physical and ecological criteria as well as social and cultural patterns resulting from human occupation of the land.

Abstract and inventive spatial thinking and problem-solving unfolds in the studio in both two and three dimensions, along with traditional in-depth academic research, analysis, and writing. The precision of craft, via the making of both two-dimensional drawings and three-dimensional models, is emphasized as an activity parallel with the precision of thinking, investigating, and problem-solving.

Catherine Seavitt-Nordenson
Third Year Landscape Design Coordinator

Danae Alessi
CATHERINE SEAVITT- NORDENSON / SCOTT SHELL, CRITICS

01

02

03

mercurial
ramps and light posts
cross bedding dune formation
moving

04

Epilogue as Prologue: Chapter IV

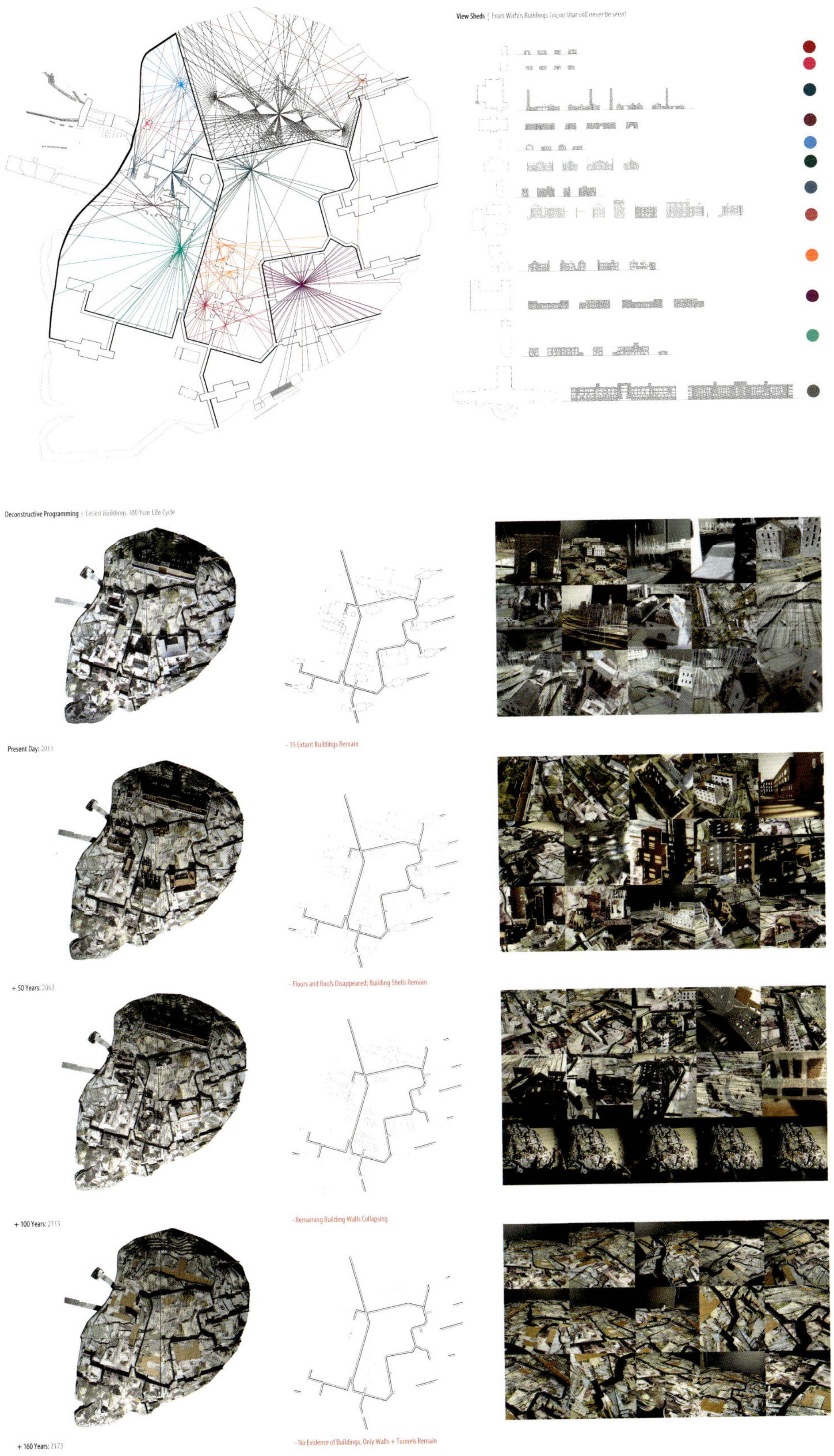

05

01, 03, 04 | Sheila Moss
02, 05 | Danae Alessi

MAST

OF SCIENCE - SUSTAINABILITY
IN THE URBAN ENVIRONMENT

ER

SUSTAINABILITY IN THE URBAN ENVIRONMENT

FACULTY
Hillary Brown

How might a small Haitian village (population +/- 1,400) lacking basic power, sanitation, waste collection and a limited water supply, achieve a measure of infrastructural self-sufficiency by relying predominantly on local resources?

This was the problem statement set out to help redevelop the farming settlement of Foché, a hamlet spread out along a main road running through Les Palmes district in the central/SW region of Haiti. Foché lies on the coast about 10 miles west from Leogane, the epicenter of the devastating January 12, 2010 earthquake. This project outlines three primary economic engines that include 1) a proposed eco-industrial park collocated within an existing gravel-crushing yard, 2) a new community center or hub proposed for the village with revenue-producing services, and 3) a new template for community-based agriculture using a permacultural approach to farming. The eco-industrial park is comprised of a concrete making facility, turning out concrete blocks for use in making village cisterns. The "Community Hub" features a cooperative computer cafe and community kitchen, a laundry facility, a clinic, and a solar-heated food-drying facility. A community scale biodigester anaerobically converts domestic organic, agricultural, human and animal waste into a fuel source (biogas) for cooking, and/or electricity co-generation, leaving a rich useable fertilizer. Basic lighting and electricity are produced by roof-top PV. Sanitation measures include the use of biodigesters for outlying homes, with composting toilets utilized near the community hub. Students identified and quantified the primary inputs and outputs, while paying attention to synergies across systems, and developed construction cost estimates and operating costs for the facilities. The results include the production of as many as 70 jobs for the village of Foché.

Hillary Brown
Director, Architecture Track
M.S. Sustainability in the Urban Environment

Miriam Ward, Teaching Assistant
HILLARY BROWN, CRITIC

2

01

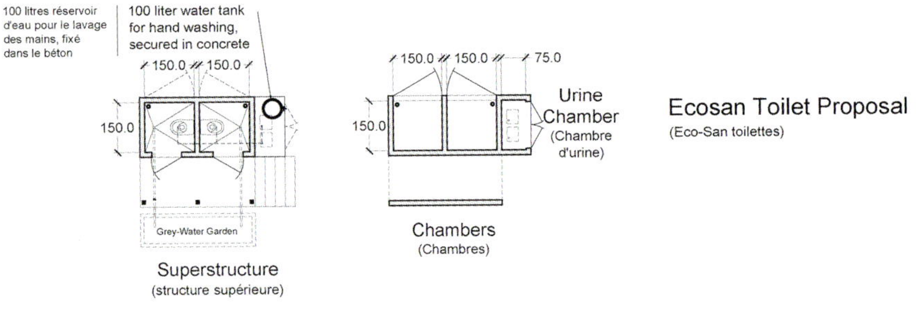
100 litres réservoir d'eau pour le lavage des mains, fixé dans le béton
100 liter water tank for hand washing, secured in concrete
150.0
150.0
150.0
Grey-Water Garden
Superstructure
(structure supérieure)
150.0
150.0
75.0
150.0
Urine Chamber
(Chambre d'urine)
Chambers
(Chambres)
Ecosan Toilet Proposal
(Eco-San toilettes)

02

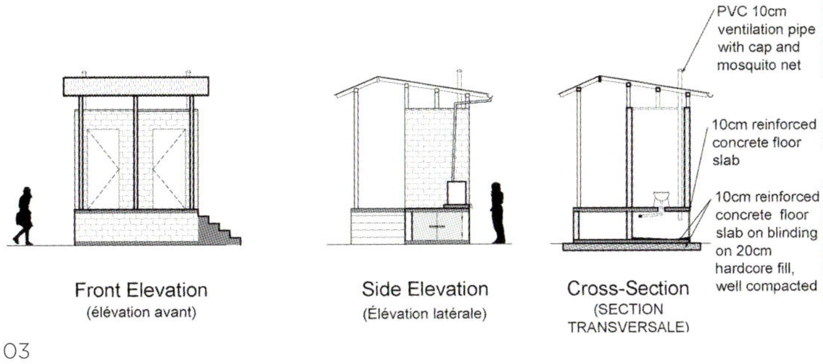

03

01-03 | William Valdez / Marina Bellini Whalen / Diana Bedoya / Jose Germosen

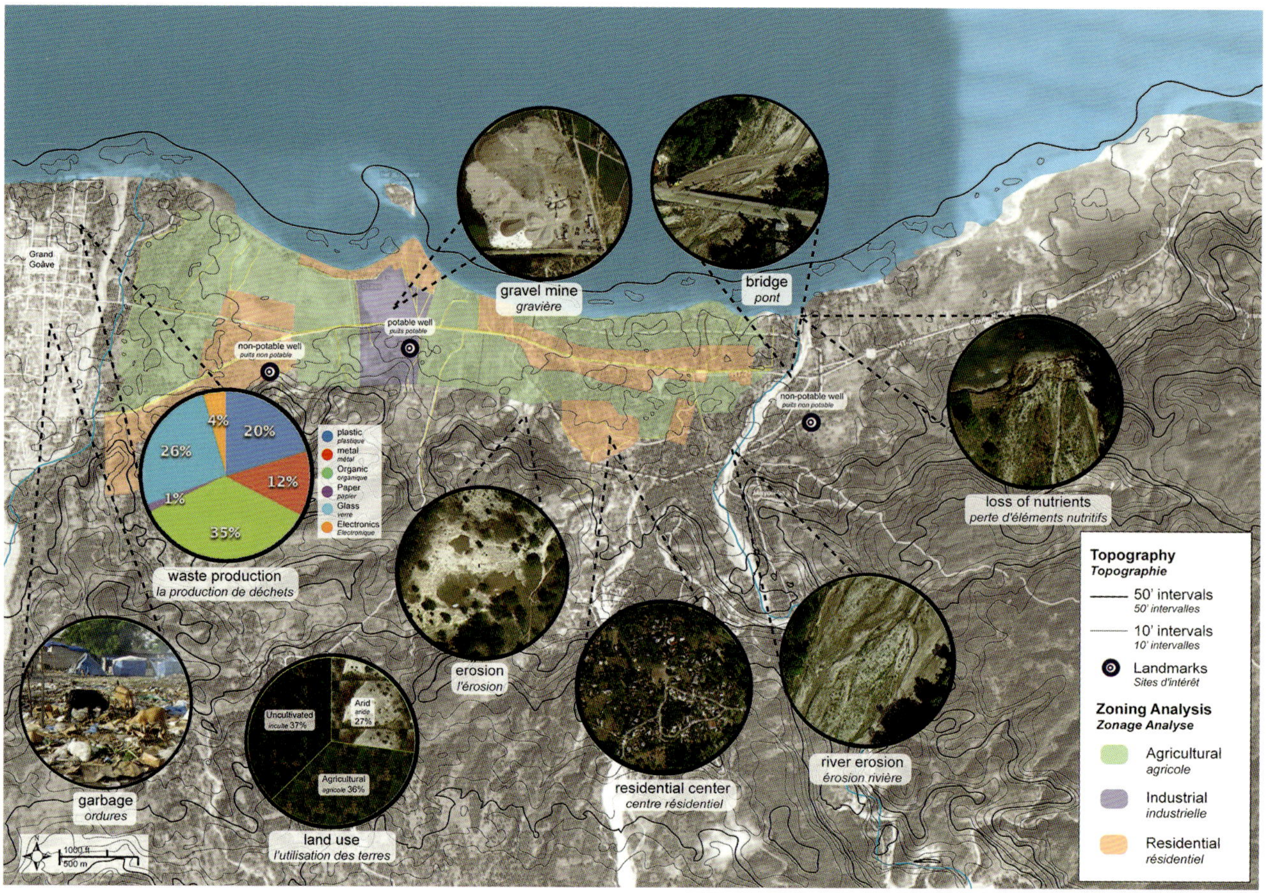
Grand Goâve
gravel mine
gravière
bridge
pont
potable well
puits potable
non-potable well
puits non potable
non-potable well
puits non potable
20%
12%
35%
1%
26%
4%
plastic
plastique
metal
métal
Organic
organique
Paper
papier
Glass
verre
Electronics
Electronique
waste production
la production de déchets
loss of nutrients
perte d'éléments nutritifs
erosion
l'érosion
residential center
centre résidentiel
river erosion
érosion rivière
garbage
ordures
Uncultivated
inculte 37%
Arid
aride
27%
Agricultural
agricole 36%
land use
l'utilisation des terres
1000 ft
500 m
Topography
Topographie
50' intervals
50' intervalles
10' intervals
10' intervalles
Landmarks
Sites d'intérêt
Zoning Analysis
Zonage Analyse
Agricultural
agricole
Industrial
industrielle
Residential
résidentiel

01

02

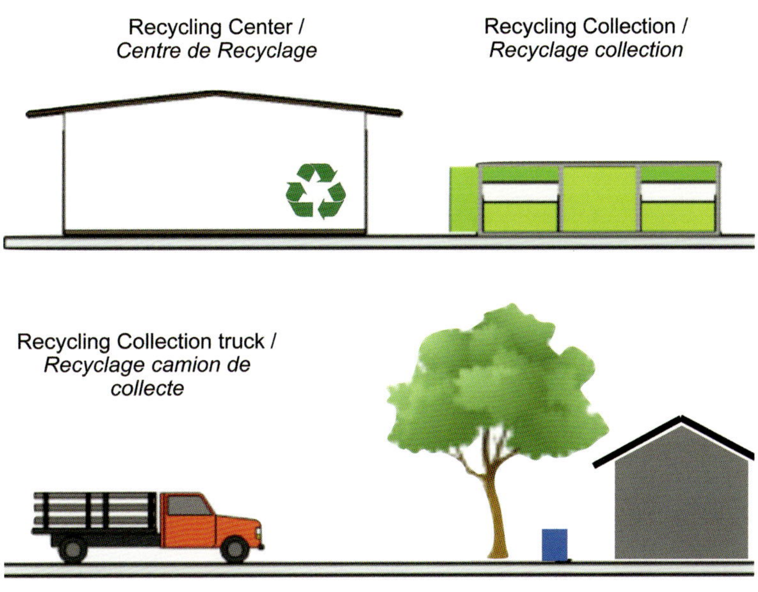

03

01, 02 | Miriam Ward
03 | Melissa Cheing

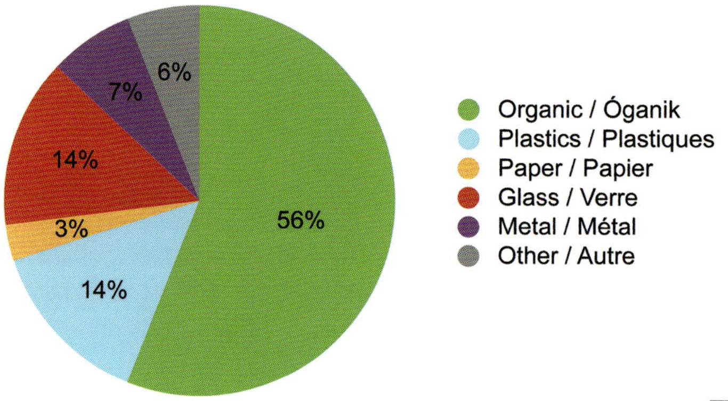

kg/day / *kg/jour*	Haiti	Grand-Goave	Fouché (75% efficiency)			
			%	Zone 1	Zone 2	Total Fouché 1390 inhabitants
Household Organic Waste / *Déchets organiques ménagers*	75%	35%	56	57.12	141.372	198.492
Human Waste / *Déchets humains*	-	-				264
Agriculture Waste / *Les déchets agricoles*	-	-				varies
Grand-Goave Market Waste / *Déchets de marché*		506.8 kg/day*				
Plastics recyclable / *Plastiques recyclables*	7%	20%	7	7.14	17.6715	24.8115
Plastics non-rec			7	7.14	17.6715	24.8115
Paper / *Papier*	5%	1%	3	3.06	7.5735	10.6335
Glass / *Verre*	2%	26%	14	14.28	35.343	49.623
Metal / *Métal*	3%	12%	7	7.14	17.6715	24.8115
Other / *Autre*	8%	4%	6	6.12	15.147	21.267

01

Sector	Initial Capital	Cost per year for Maintenance	Short-term Jobs	Long-term Jobs
A **District Biodigester** *district biodigesteur*	$ 56,000.00	$ 8,000.00	10	5
B **Community Hub** *hub communauté*	$ 118,500.00	$ 9,600.00	20	12
C **Residential Zone** *zone résidentielle*	$ 70,400.00	$ 5,500.00	15	8
D **Eco-Industrial Park** *Parc éco-industrielle*	$ 76,300.00	$ 15,600.00	5	5
E **Energy Generation** *production d'énergie*	$ 31,600.00	$ 3,500.00	5	2
F **Water Infrastructure** *Infrastructures de l'eau*	$ 40,200.00	$ 11,100.00	20	10
G **Agroforestry** *agroforesterie*	$ 42,300.00	$ 9,700.00	15	28
Total	**$ 491,300.00**	**$ 71,000.00**	**100**	**75**

Calculations Summary
Résumé des calculs

Fouché, Haiti

02

03

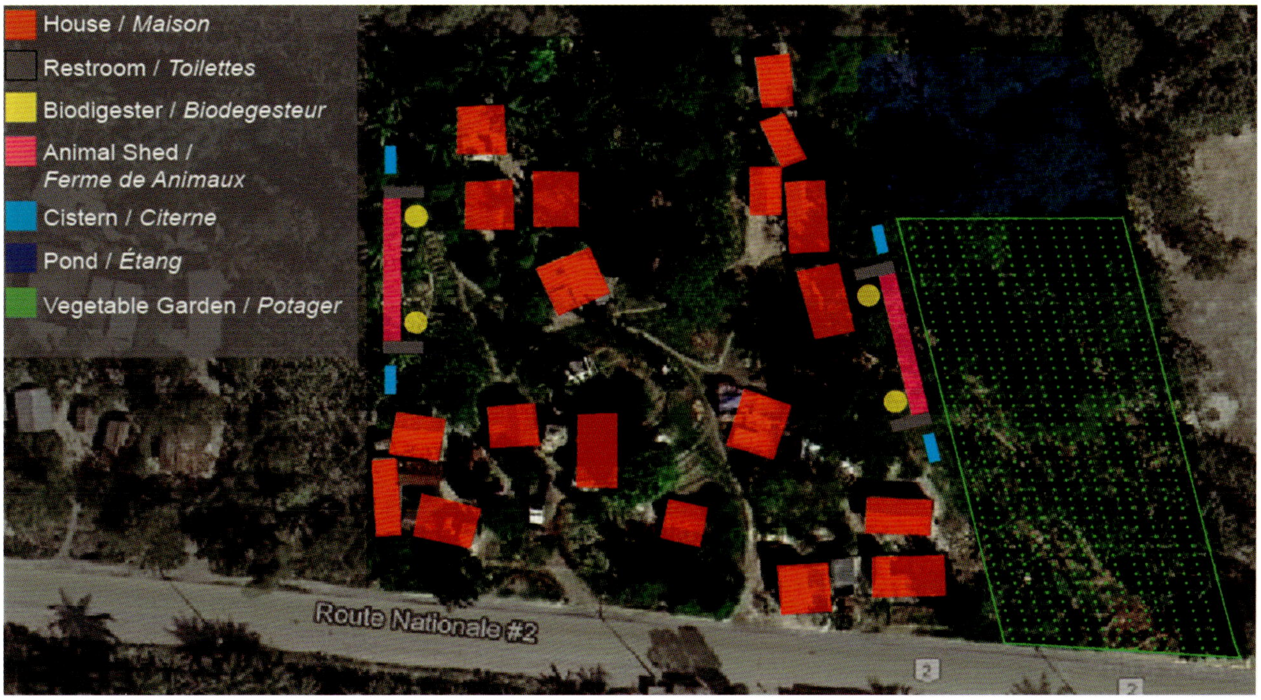

04

01, 02 | Melissa Cheing / Arthur Getman / Tyler Partato
03, 04 | Miriam Ward / Arthur Munoz Hansen / Shanshan Lee

VISUA
STUDI

VISUAL REPRESENTATION

L

ES

VISUAL STUDIES

FACULTY
Bradley Horn / Elisabetta Terragni / Michael Szivos / Alvaro Soto / Albert Vecerka / Irma L. Ostroff / Lewis Iglehart

Critical to any architecture student's success in the field is their ability to accurately and expressively represent both what they think and what they see. Visual Representation courses at the Spitzer School of Architecture augment and extend the lessons learned in design studio courses and cover a wide range of skills from free-hand drawing to digital rendering to projection drawing. Represented here is a sampling of these courses.

In Visual Studies, students are taught advanced rendering techniques as well as a range of other skills including digital photomontage and a critical approach to historical forms of representation. In Advanced Computing students use generative modeling to explore fabrication at a range of scales. In Architecture and Photography students learn how to master digital tools of photography and editing. In Discovering Form in Nature students learn the valuable lesson of free-hand life-drawing.

Bradley Horn
Visual Studies Coordinator

Christos Athanassiou / Nicholas Cichanowski
MICHAEL SZIVOS, CRITIC

01

02

03

04

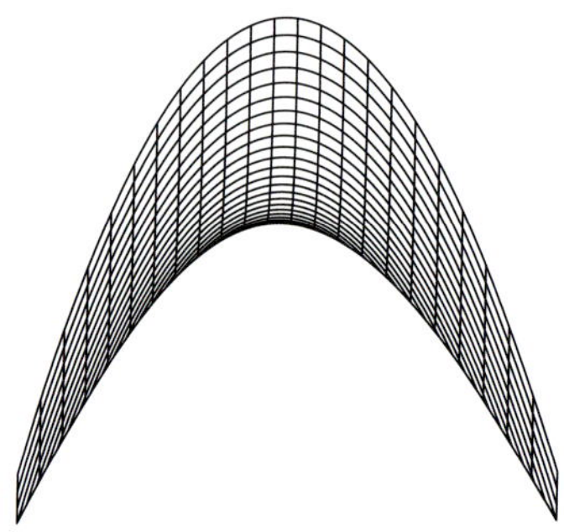
05

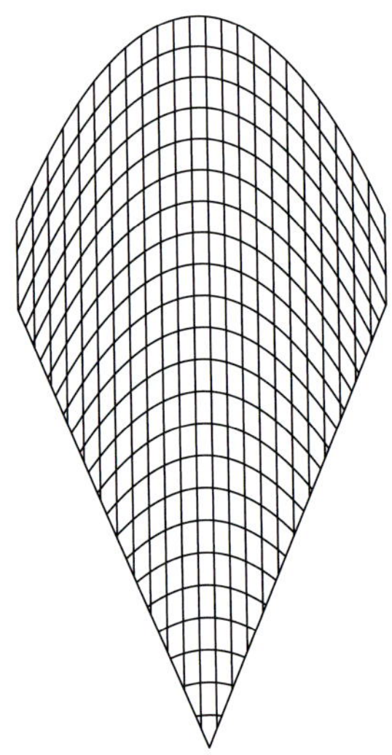
06

07

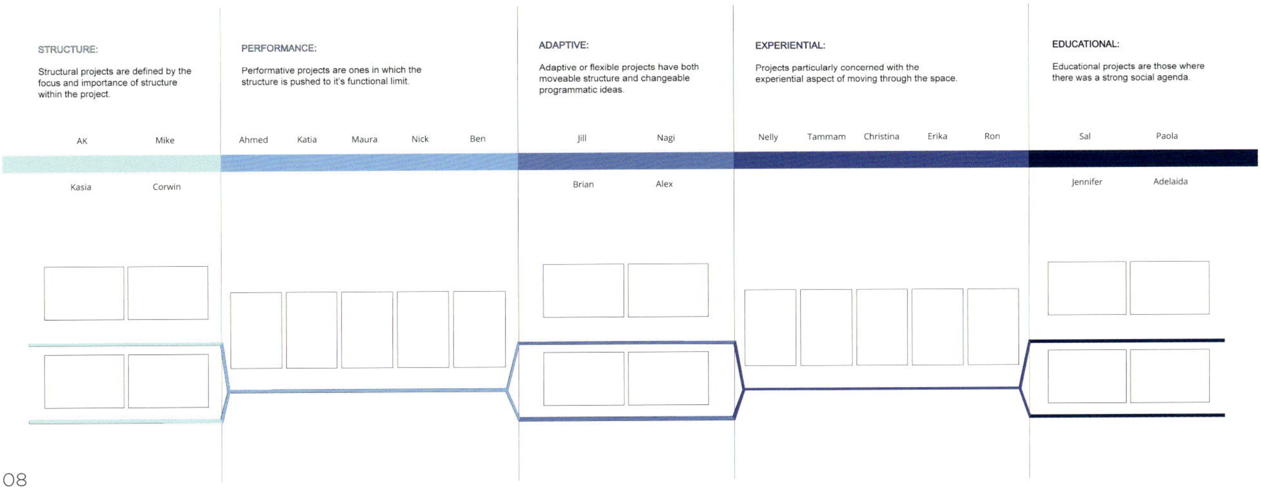

08

09

01, 02 | Adelaida Baez-Urena / Christina Hernandez / Paola Martinez / Ronald Martin / Alexander La Ferla
03 | Jennifer Ewald / Jill Bunyea / Katerina Marcelja / Maura Whang / Ahmed Dirhalleh / Salvatore Cosenza
04-06 | Kasia Wilusz / Lyubov Tsinis / Benjamin Tulman / Brian Lantz / Nicholas Friedmann
07-09 | Jennifer Ewald / Jill Bunyea / Katerina Marcelja / Maura Whang / Ahmed Dirhalleh / Salvatore Cosenza / Corwin Carroll / Kasia Wilusz / Lyubov Tsinis / Benjamin Tulman / Brian Lantz / Michael Joseph / Mohammed Tammam Munir / Adelaida Baez-Urena / Christina Hernandez / Paola Martinez / Ronald Martin / Bantwal Akshay Mallya / Alexander La Ferla / Nagi Alamri / Nan Li / Nelly Sachakova / Nicholas Friedmann

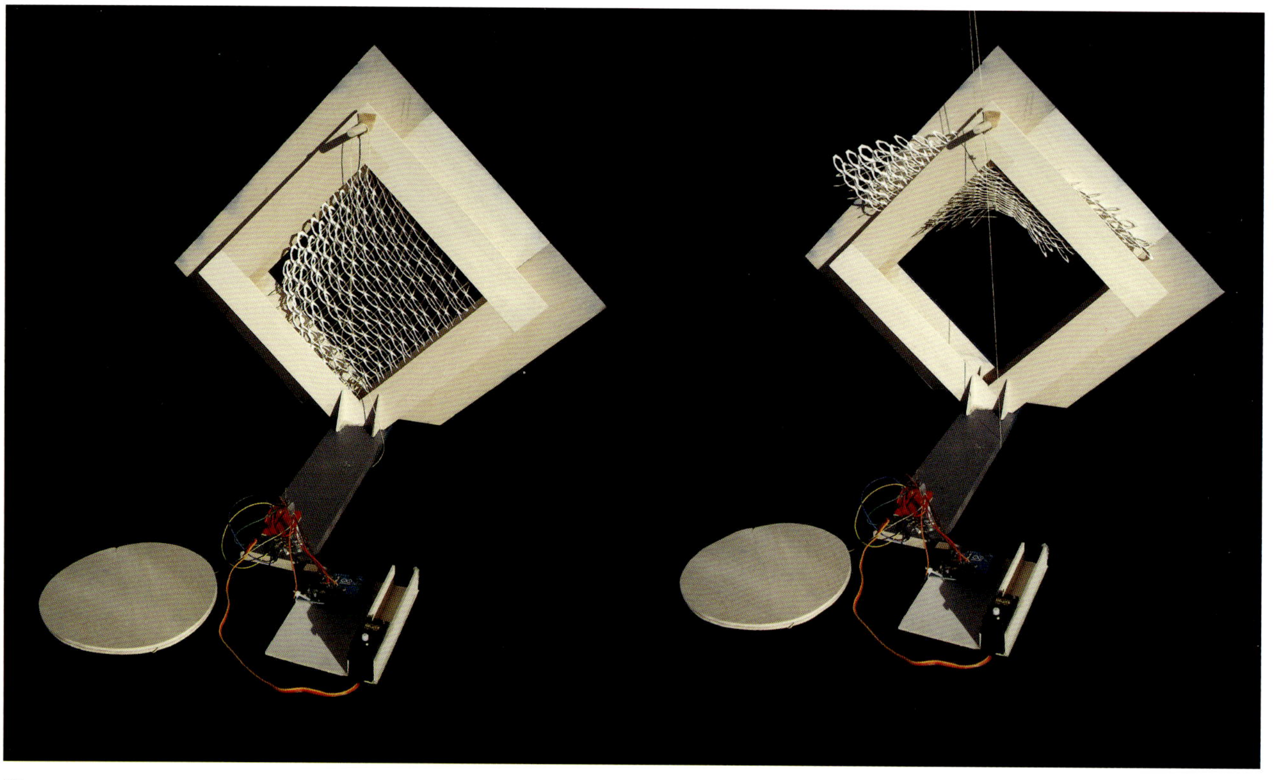

01

02

03

04

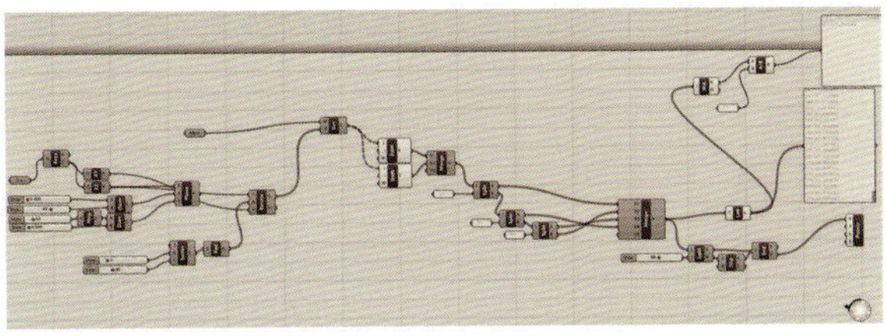

05

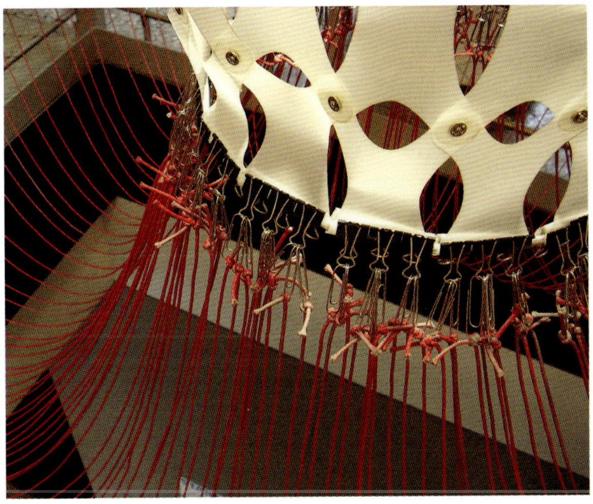

06

07

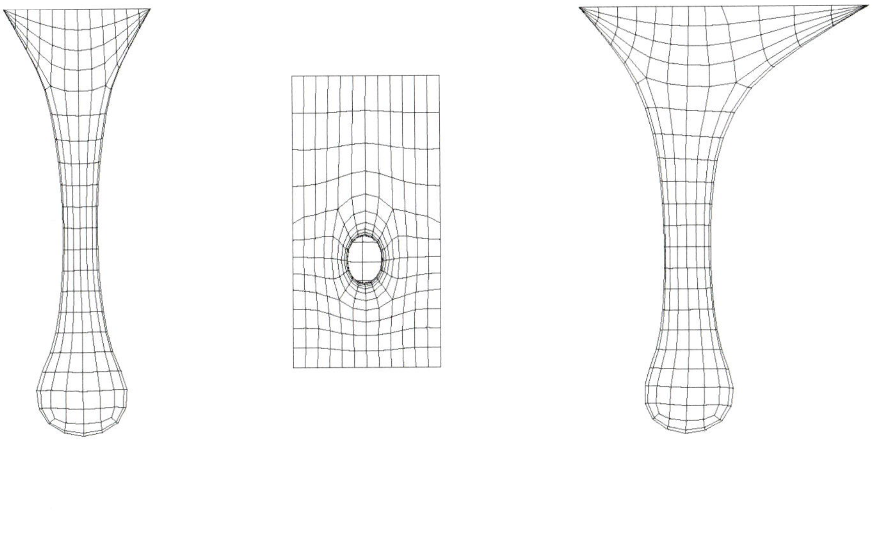

08

01 | Laura Sanburn / Julian Henderson
02-04 | Gregory Nakata / Chad Richardson
05-07 | Luke Weinstock / David Butterini
08 | Christos Athanassiou / Nicholas Cichanowski

01

02

03

04

05

06

01 | Idan Saragosti
02 | Enoch Mariscal
03 | David Franck / Isaac Selolwane / Nan Li
04 | Michael Warshaw
05 | Stephanie Paul
06 | Tortajad Diaz / Lou Gemma

01

02

03

04

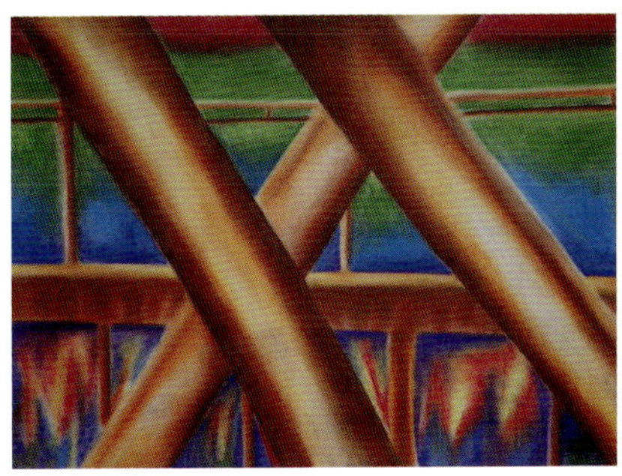

05

01-02 | Jose Jimenez
03 | Roshini Jhagru
04 | Jasmine Ibrahim
05 | Susan Wu

DAVID WERBER

TRAVE
FELLO

IN BARCELONA 2012 - 2013

LING
WSHIP

DAVID WERBER TRAVELING FELLOWSHIP IN BARCELONA

FACULTY
Fabian Llonch

The David Werber Traveling Fellowship Summer Program offers a four-week intensive architectural design studio, which takes place in the city of Barcelona, Spain. This CCNY summer program engages a group of 10 advanced students in a concentrated architectural experience, while taking a clear approach of interacting with the City of Barcelona, its unique architecture, people and culture. This experience, in such an exciting city, proves to have a tremendous impact on their architectural education, especially at the stage in which they are at.

With the studio at its core, the program will be as exciting and dynamic as the city in which it takes place. The studio will be affiliated with the local school of architecture; The Escola Tècnica Superior d'Arquitectura de Barcelona (ETSAB). Students participating in the program will receive four elective credits during summer course at CCNY.

The exercise this summer was a hybrid between the Exhibition Space for the Escola Massana and La Boqueria Restaurant. Understanding the proximity and the synergy between El Mercado La Boqueria and La Escola Massana is to comprehend the particularity of the site. All mixed in between the vibrant neighborhood of el Raval. The project should enable us to learn, to enjoy, to discover, to taste, to look... life itself.

Fabian Llonch
Studio Coordinator

EMPORAN DE BARCE

01

02

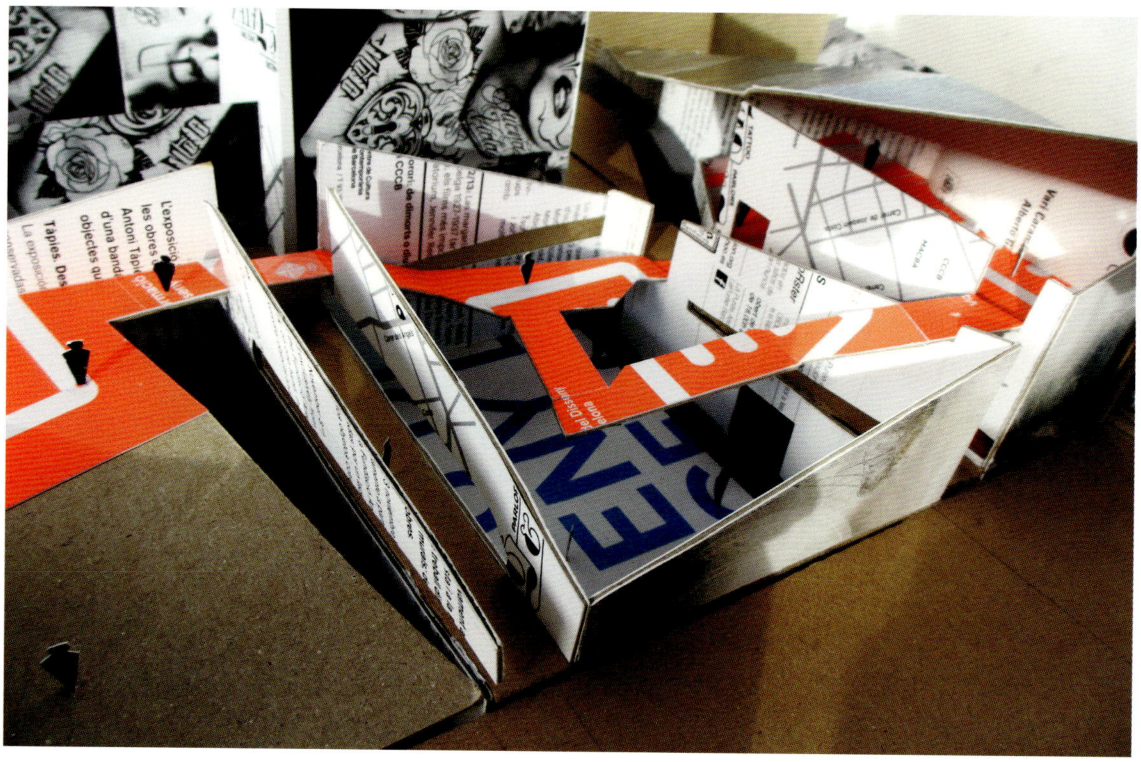

03

04

05

07

06

08

01 | Jeffery Bermudez
02 | Anthony Giron
03 | Vail Nuguid
04 | Veronica Rivas
05 | Mary Rizaldo
06 | Melinda Siew
07 | Jessica Tseng
08 | Jacline Vargas
09 | Leanne Zick
10 | Matthew Mblamely

SPITZER

TRAVE
GRAN

L

T 2012

SPITZER TRAVEL GRANT 2012

Since 2010, sixteen graduates of the Spitzer School of Architecture have studied architecture, urbanism, and landscape architecture in places all over the world. Proposing to work solo or in teams, these students competed for a $5,000 travel grant that is named after the architecture school's benefactors, Bernard and Anne Spitzer. It is thanks to Spitzer's generosity that the SSA is able to encourage undergraduate and graduate students to travel and study abroad in the year following graduation. The goal is to enable SSA graduates not only to experience different cultures but also to develop their knowledge of how culture, history and environment influence architecture, urban design and landscape architecture and incorporate that understanding and research skills into practice. Previous recipients have visited Spain, Japan, Mexico, Turkey, Italy, Sri Lanka, Myanmar, Indonesia, Cambodia, Colombia, and the United States.

Marta Gutman
Spitzer Travel Fellowship Coordinator

Sin Agua
Fragmented Realities of an Evaporating Hyper-Metropolis

Winning the Spitzer School of Architecture's Traveling Fellowship gave us the opportunity to visit and reside in Mexico City for a summer. After spending countless days in the rain and learning that most of the runoff would never be recycled, we decided to propose a local solution to the city's dire water predicament. Because of the overwhelming presence and heavy dependency of food stalls and carts, we began to see them as vital pieces of infrastructure rather than informal eyesore sheds. Our proposal was to reinvent the food stall as natural filtering "planter boxes" that would provide a direct water source for street vendors. These concrete cores would utilize the biosand filtering method, a natural and easily maintained filtration system, used in countries where potable water is inaccessible.

Jamie Silvestro / Michael Ong
Fifth Semester Design

DE
OS VIEJOS
O FEDERAL
FDJ
CE.

01

02

03

04

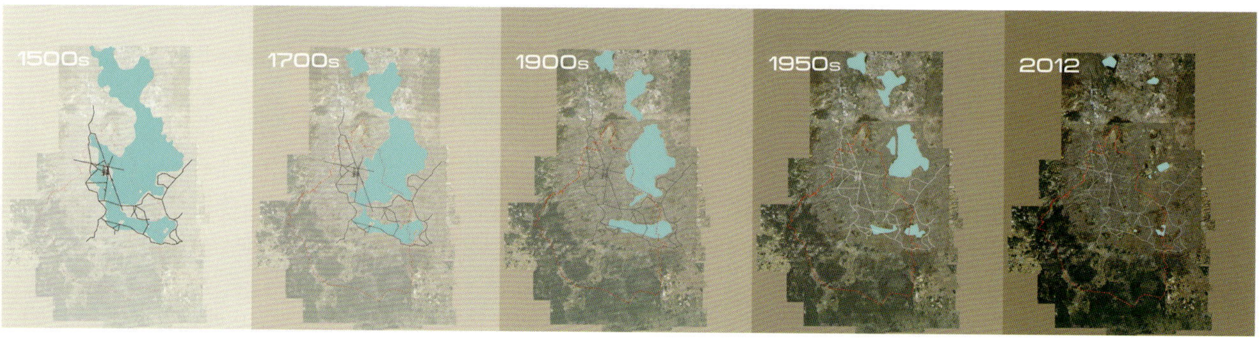

05

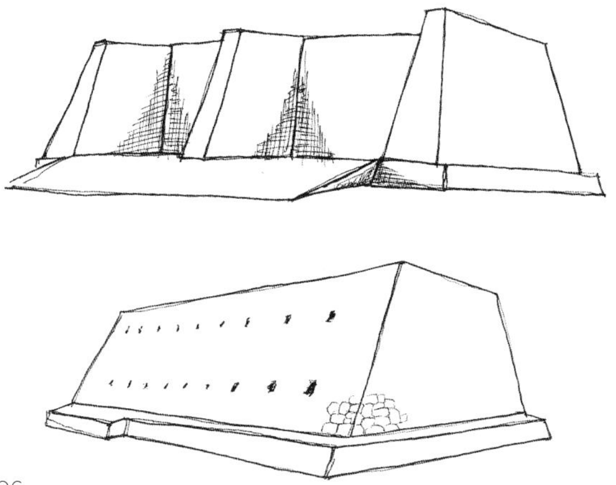

06

08

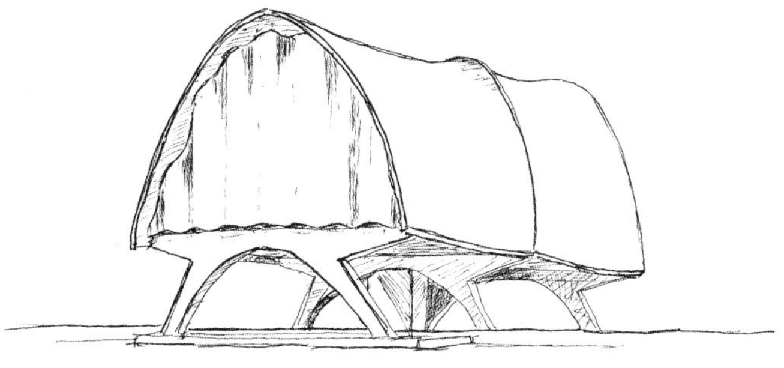

07

09

01-09 | Jamie Silvestro / Michael Ong

LECTU
EVENT

2012-2013

RES &
S

A LINE AROUND AN IDEA

An Exhibition of Hand Drawings by James Wines for SITE

September 20, 2012 – April 5, 2013

Opening Reception: Thursday, September 20, 2012
6:00PM – 8:00PM

Atrium Gallery
The Bernard and Anne Spitzer School of Architecture

Gallery Hours, 9:00AM – 6:00PM

The City College of New York
141 Convent Avenue (at 135th Street) New York, NY 10031

GALLERY
A line around an idea

01

02

03

04

05

01 | Audrey Matlock's Studio: Bradley Horn / Lance Jay Brown / Stephen Dynia / Illya Azaroff / Mark Regulinski / Student: Timothy Miron
02 | Catherine Seavitt-Nordenson / Mersiha Veledar Joint Studio: Charles McKinney / Achva Benzinberg Stein / Nathaniel Harris / Lee Weintraub / Student: Eli Sands
03 | Yolande Daniels' Studio: Alice Chun / Galia Solomonoff / Julio Salcedo-Fernandez / Juliette Spertus / Karla Rothstein / Kaja Kühl / Bradley Horn / Rob Lane / Catherine Seavitt-Nordenson / Student: Michael Luft-Weissberg
04 | Lee Weintraub / Julio Salcedo-Fernandez / Peter Gisolfi Joint Studio: Carmi Bee / Robert Garneau / Catherine Seavitt-Nordenson / John Clarke / Mark Ginsberg / Yehre Suh / Students: Rebecca Dorff / Shelley Yang
05 | Elisabetta Terragni's Studio: Kenneth Frampton / Kurt W. Forster / Suzan Wines / Student: Chang Youl Han

01

02

03

04

01 | Elisabetta Terragni's Studio: Marta Gutman / Toni L. Griffin / James Lowder / Martin Stigsgaard / Student: Maura Whang
02 | Nandini Bagchee's Studio: Lauren Jacobi / David Holson / Sara Jacinto / Christian Volkmann / Ali Hocek / Student: Lenny Chen
03 | Catherine Seavitt-Nordenson / Scott Shell Joint Studio: Matthew McMahon / Wolfram Hoefer / David Hays / Student: Anamel Sanchez Lee
04 | Michael Sorkin's Studio: June Williamson / Quilian Riano / Einat Manoff / Marshall Berman / Michael Parkinson / Paolo Genovese / Student: David Lee

BERNARD AND ANNE SPITZER SCHOOL OF ARCHITECTURE THE CITY COLLEGE OF NEW YORK/CUNY

Sciame Lecture Series Fall 2012

ART, ARCHITECTURE AND THE LANDSCAPE

9/6 **JOHN HONG/JINHEE PARK**
SsD Works

9/13 **JOSEPH TANNEY**
Current Preoccupations

9/27 **JAMES WINES**
A Line Around an Idea

10/4 **CHRISTO**
Christo and Jeanne-Claude, Two Works in Progress

10/11 **URSULA von RYDINGSVARD**
Sculpture

10/18 **LIU KECHENG**
Going Through Historical Space

11/1 **ALICE AYCOCK**
Alice Aycock: Selected Works

11/15 **MARY MISS**
City as Living Laboratory: Sustainability Made Tangible Through the Arts

All lectures will be held at 6:30 pm in the Bernard and Anne Spitzer School of Architecture Sciame Auditorium 141 Convent Avenue (at W. 135th Street) New York, NY 10031 T. 212 650 7118 All lectures are free and open to the public. Lectures are now simulcast and archived on the web at www.ccny.cuny.edu/ssa

Lecture series sponsored by

Sciame... WHERE BUILDING IS AN ART

F.J. Sciame Construction Co., Inc. 14 Wall Street, New York, NY 10005
Information on continuing education credits for licensed NYS architects call: 212 650 7118

the City College of New York

CITY COLLEGE IS CUNY

BERNARD AND ANNE SPITZER SCHOOL OF ARCHITECTURE THE CITY COLLEGE OF NEW YORK/CUNY

Sciame Lecture Series Spring 2013

RETHINKING KAHN

1/31	**CARTER WISEMAN** *Louis I. Kahn: Beyond Time and Style*
2/7	**SARAH WILLIAMS GOLDHAGEN** *Louis Kahn, Yesterday and Today*
2/21	**ROBERT McCARTER** *Demanding Presence: The Unbuilt Works of Louis I. Kahn*
2/28	**STANISLAUS VON MOOS** *Monument? Forum? Fair? - On Kahn's Urbanism Today*
3/7	**KENNETH FRAMPTON** *Modernity and Monumentality in the works of Louis Kahn*
3/21	**GINA POLLARA** *In Motion & Repose: Louis Kahn's Memorial to Franklin D. Roosevelt*
4/4	**ROBERT TWOMBLY** *What Will Be Has Always Been*
4/11	**WILLIAM JR CURTIS** *The Space of Ideas*

All lectures will be held at 6:30 pm in the Bernard and Anne Spitzer School of Architecture Sciame Auditorium 141 Convent Avenue (at W. 135th Street) New York, NY 10031 T. 212 650 7118
All lectures are free and open to the public.
Lectures are now simulcast and archived on the web at www.ccny.cuny.edu/ssa

Lecture series sponsored by
Sciame... WHERE BUILDING IS AN ART
F.J. Sciame Construction Co., Inc. 14 Wall Street, New York, NY 10005
Information on continuing education credits for licensed NYS architects call: 212 650 7118
The Ninth Annual Lewis Mumford Lecture on Urbanism with speaker Marshall Berman will be held on Thursday, May 2, 2013 at 6:30pm. The Great Hall of Shepard Hall, City College of New York

the City College of New York

CITY COLLEGE IS CUNY

Maintaining the Long View
A Conversation Between
William J.R. Curtis
and
George Ranalli
Friday, April 12th
11:00 - 1:00
Reception to Follow
Sciame Auditorium
Bernard and Anne Spitzer
School of Architectture
The City College of the
City University of New York
Photo: William J.R. Curtis, 1996

The City College of New York
THURSDAY
MAY
SECOND
2013
6:30PM
Marshall Berman
The Graduate Program in Urban Design
Bernard and Anne Spitzer School of Architecture
CITY COLLEGE OF NEW YORK
is pleased to announce the ninth annual
Lewis Mumford Lecture on Urbanism
The Great Hall of Shepard Hall, CCNY, Convent Avenue at 138th Street, New York, NY
This lecture is free and open to the public. No reservations are necessary.
EMERGING
FROM
THE
RUINS
ART DIRECTION: BEYMAN STUDIO PHOTO: OFER BILIK

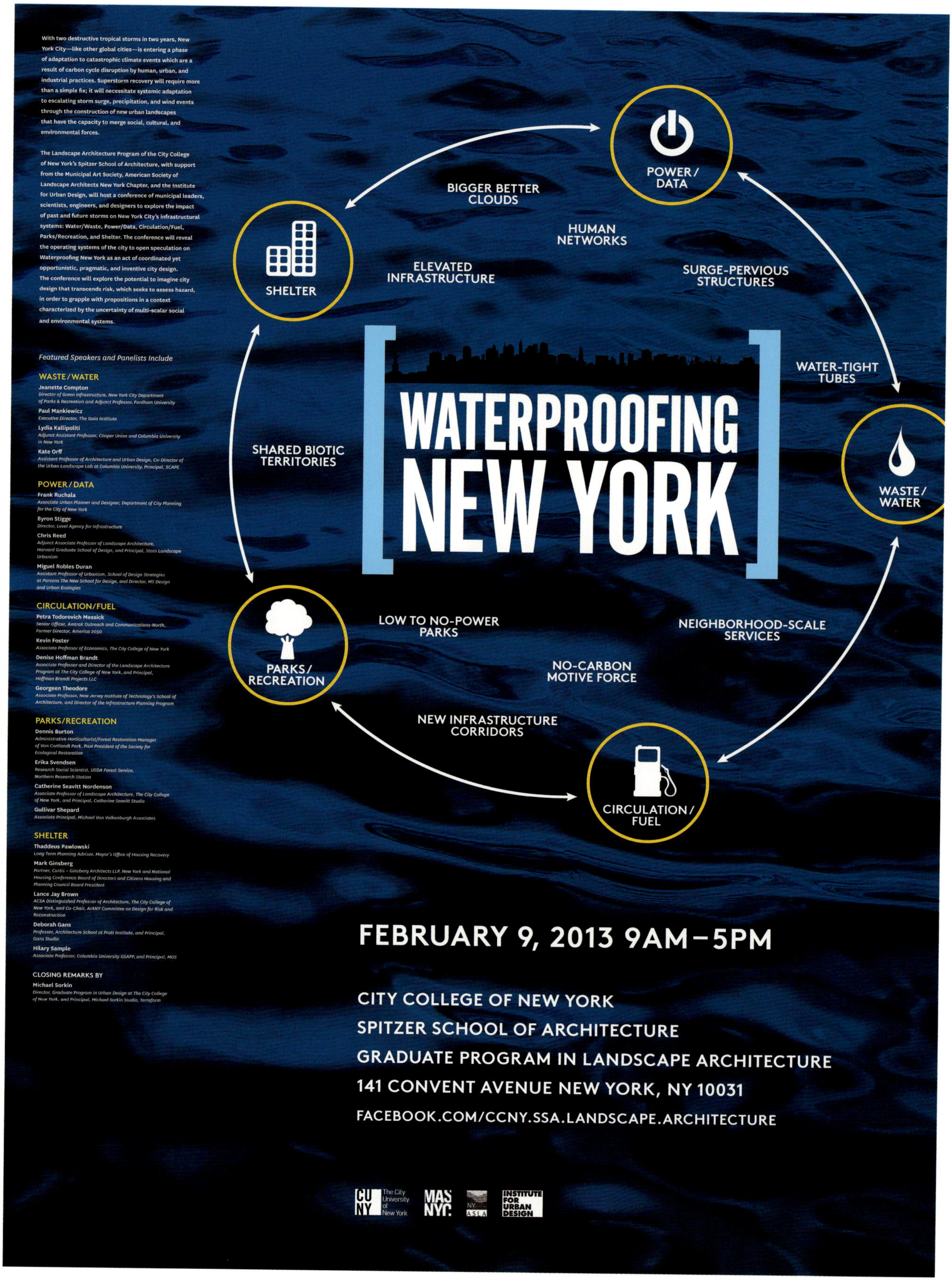
With two destructive tropical storms in two years, New York City—like other global cities—is entering a phase of adaptation to catastrophic climate events which are a result of carbon cycle disruption by human, urban, and industrial practices. Superstorm recovery will require more than a simple fix; it will necessitate systemic adaptation to escalating storm surge, precipitation, and wind events through the construction of new urban landscapes that have the capacity to merge social, cultural, and environmental forces.
The Landscape Architecture Program of the City College of New York's Spitzer School of Architecture, with support from the Municipal Art Society, American Society of Landscape Architects New York Chapter, and the Institute for Urban Design, will host a conference of municipal leaders, scientists, engineers, and designers to explore the impact of past and future storms on New York City's infrastructural systems: Water/Waste, Power/Data, Circulation/Fuel, Parks/Recreation, and Shelter. The conference will reveal the operating systems of the city to open speculation on Waterproofing New York as an act of coordinated yet opportunistic, pragmatic, and inventive city design. The conference will explore the potential to imagine city design that transcends risk, which seeks to assess hazard, in order to grapple with propositions in a context characterized by the uncertainty of multi-scalar social and environmental systems.
Featured Speakers and Panelists Include
WASTE / WATER
Jeanette Compton
Director of Green Infrastructure, New York City Department of Parks & Recreation and Adjunct Professor, Fordham University
Paul Mankiewicz
Executive Director, The Gaia Institute
Lydia Kallipoliti
Adjunct Assistant Professor, Cooper Union and Columbia University in New York
Kate Orff
Assistant Professor of Architecture and Urban Design, Co-Director of the Urban Landscape Lab at Columbia University, Principal, SCAPE
POWER / DATA
Frank Ruchala
Associate Urban Planner and Designer, Department of City Planning for the City of New York
Byron Stigge
Director, Level Agency for Infrastructure
Chris Reed
Adjunct Associate Professor of Landscape Architecture, Harvard Graduate School of Design, and Principal, Stoss Landscape Urbanism
Miguel Robles Duran
Assistant Professor of Urbanism, School of Design Strategies at Parsons The New School for Design, and Director, MS Design and Urban Ecologies
CIRCULATION/FUEL
Petra Todorovich Messick
Senior Officer, Amtrak Outreach and Communications-North, Former Director, America 2050
Kevin Foster
Associate Professor of Economics, The City College of New York
Denise Hoffman Brandt
Associate Professor and Director of the Landscape Architecture Program at The City College of New York, and Principal, Hoffman Brandt Projects LLC
Georgeen Theodore
Associate Professor, New Jersey Institute of Technology's School of Architecture, and Director of the Infrastructure Planning Program
PARKS/RECREATION
Dennis Burton
Administrative Horticulturist/Forest Restoration Manager of Van Cortlandt Park, Past President of the Society for Ecological Restoration
Erika Svendsen
Research Social Scientist, USDA Forest Service, Northern Research Station
Catherine Seavitt Nordenson
Associate Professor of Landscape Architecture, The City College of New York, and Principal, Catherine Seavitt Studio
Gullivar Shepard
Associate Principal, Michael Van Valkenburgh Associates
SHELTER
Thaddeus Pawlowski
Long Term Planning Advisor, Mayor's Office of Housing Recovery
Mark Ginsberg
Partner, Curtis + Ginsberg Architects LLP, New York and National Housing Conference Board of Directors and Citizens Housing and Planning Council Board President
Lance Jay Brown
ACSA Distinguished Professor of Architecture, The City College of New York, and Co-Chair, AIANY Committee on Design for Risk and Reconstruction
Deborah Gans
Professor, Architecture School at Pratt Institute, and Principal, Gans Studio
Hilary Sample
Associate Professor, Columbia University GSAPP, and Principal, MOS
CLOSING REMARKS BY
Michael Sorkin
Director, Graduate Program in Urban Design at The City College of New York, and Principal, Michael Sorkin Studio, Terreform
POWER / DATA
BIGGER BETTER CLOUDS
HUMAN NETWORKS
SHELTER
ELEVATED INFRASTRUCTURE
SURGE-PERVIOUS STRUCTURES
WATER-TIGHT TUBES
WATERPROOFING NEW YORK
SHARED BIOTIC TERRITORIES
WASTE / WATER
LOW TO NO-POWER PARKS
NEIGHBORHOOD-SCALE SERVICES
PARKS / RECREATION
NO-CARBON MOTIVE FORCE
NEW INFRASTRUCTURE CORRIDORS
CIRCULATION / FUEL
FEBRUARY 9, 2013 9AM–5PM
CITY COLLEGE OF NEW YORK
SPITZER SCHOOL OF ARCHITECTURE
GRADUATE PROGRAM IN LANDSCAPE ARCHITECTURE
141 CONVENT AVENUE NEW YORK, NY 10031
FACEBOOK.COM/CCNY.SSA.LANDSCAPE.ARCHITECTURE
CUNY The City University of New York
MAS NYC
NY ASLA
INSTITUTE FOR URBAN DESIGN

BEYOND WATERPROOFING

MAY 10, 2013
5–7:30PM

WASTE / WATER · CIRCULATION / FUEL · POWER / DATA · PARKS / RECREATION · SHELTER

The Landscape Architecture Program of the City College of New York's Spitzer School of Architecture, with support from the Municipal Art Society, American Society of Landscape Architects New York Chapter, and the Institute for Urban Design, will host the follow-up presentation to the March 2, 2013 conference of municipal leaders, scientists, engineers, and designers exploring the impact of past and future storms on New York City's infrastructural systems: Water/Waste, Power/Data, Circulation/Fuel, Parks/Recreation, and Shelter.

This event will present the designer-participants' approach to re-imagining the operating systems of the city in order to waterproof New York, featuring:

Deborah Gans
Denise Hoffman Brandt
Lydia Kallipoliti
Kate Orff
Chris Reed
Miguel Robles Duran
Hilary Sample
Catherine Seavitt Nordenson
Michael Sorkin
Gullivar Shepard
Georgeen Theodore

FRIDAY, MAY 10, 2013
5–7:30PM
City College of New York
Spitzer School of Architecture
Graduate Program in Landscape Architecture
141 Convent Avenue
New York, NY 10031

More information online at
FACEBOOK.COM/CCNY.SSA.LANDSCAPE.ARCHITECTURE

CUNY The City University of New York · MAS NYC · NY ASLA · INSTITUTE FOR URBAN DESIGN

NY13 PASSIVE HOUSE symposium

POLICY FINANCE PERFORMANCE

2ND ANNUAL NEW YORK PASSIVE HOUSE SYMPOSIUM

Saturday, June 8th
8:30am - 5:15pm

City College of New York, The Bernard & Anne Spitzer School of Architecture

www.nypassivehouse.org

SSA MASTER OF ARCHITECTURE *CONVERSATIONS WITH STUDENTS* LECTURE SERIES / SPRING 2013

THE IMPOSSIBLE ATLAS

February 25
Kurt W. Forster
Distinguished Professor, Director of Doctoral Studies at Yale University School of Architecture
Historian, Critic, Writer

"I don't remember, I don't recall... NOTHING AT ALL" (David Byrne)
Loose Sheets from Warburg's Atlas of Memory

March 18
Meredith Tenhoor
Associate Professor, Pratt Institute School of Architecture
Chair, the Aggregate Architectural History Collaborative

Accounting for Change

April 8
Cameron Tonkinwise
Director of Design Studies
School of Design, Carnegie Mellon University

Being Serviced, By People or Things

April 15
Catie Newell
Founding Principal of *Alibi Studio
Assistant Professor of Architecture, Taubman College, University of Michigan

Whereabouts

April 22
Kiel Moe
Assistant Professor of Architectural Technology, Harvard Graduate School of Design
Director, Energy, Environments & Design Research Lab

Maximum Power Design

All lectures take place on Mondays in room 128 at 7pm.

PLOT
FALL 2012
MON SEPT 10
THE PAWNBROKER
Directed by Sidney Lumet, 1964
116 minutes
INTRODUCED BY SHEILA MOSS
MON OCT 15
SPIRITED AWAY
Directed by Hayao Miyazaki, 2001
125 minutes
INTRODUCED BY MICHAEL MASON
MON SEPT 24
CHINATOWN
Directed by Roman Polanski, 1974
130 minutes
INTRODUCED BY TYLER SILVESTRO
MON OCT 22
CITY OF GOD
Directed by Fernando Meirelles, 2002
130 minutes
INTRODUCED BY KELLY MCCRACKEN
MON OCT 1
PARIS IS BURNING
Directed by Jenny Livingston, 1990
71 minutes
INTRODUCED BY CATHERINE SEAVITT
MON OCT 29
MAN ON WIRE
Directed by James Marsh, 2008
94 minutes
INTRODUCED BY STUART POLASKY
ROOFTOP CINEMA
SPITZER SCHOOL OF ARCHITECTURE
MONDAY NIGHTS AT 7:00PM
FREE AND OPEN TO ALL CITY COLLEGE STUDENTS, FACULTY, STAFF, AND FRIENDS
The City College of New York

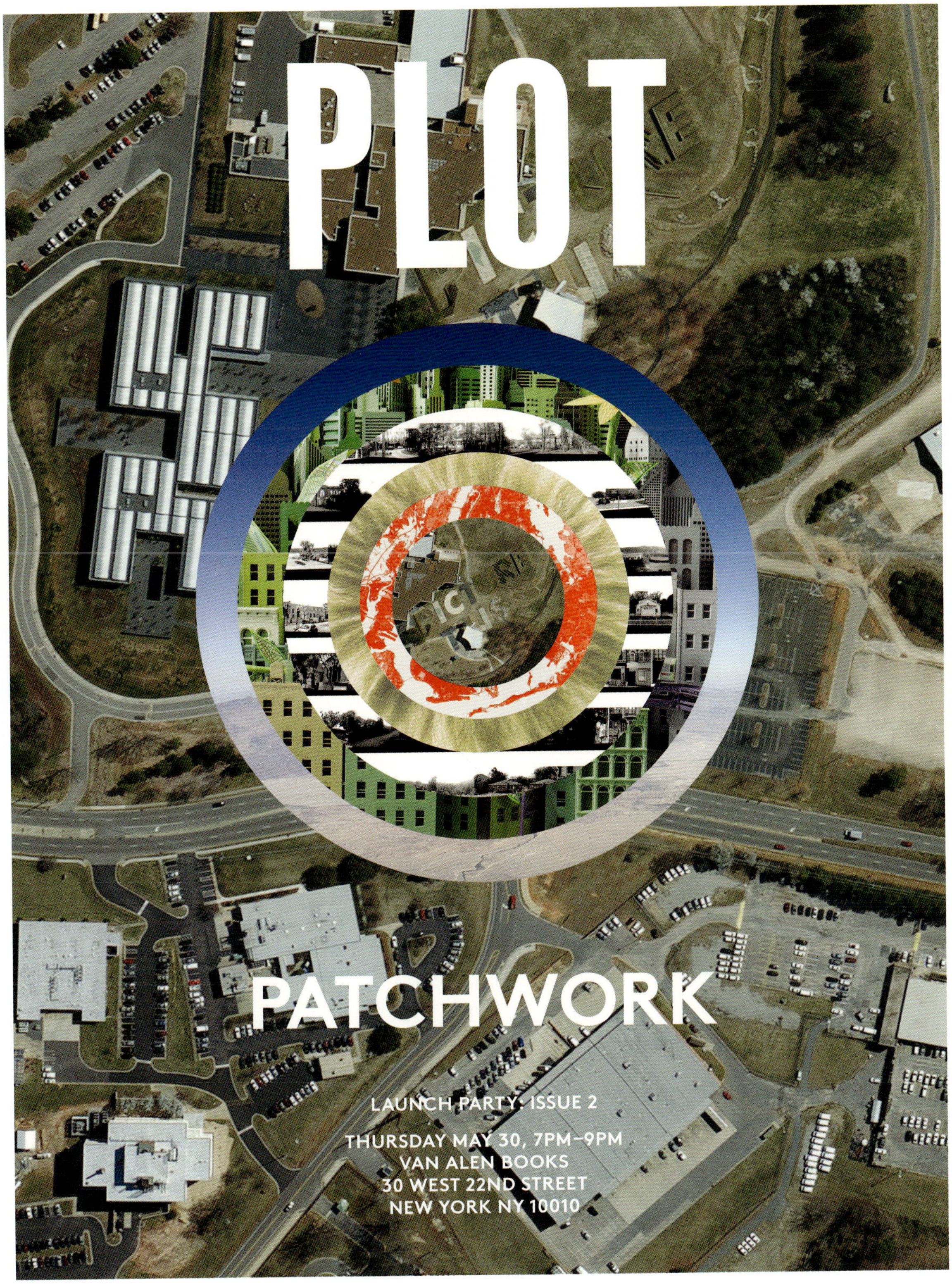
PLOT
PATCHWORK
LAUNCH PARTY: ISSUE 2
THURSDAY MAY 30, 7PM–9PM
VAN ALEN BOOKS
30 WEST 22ND STREET
NEW YORK NY 10010

YALE
UNIVERSITY
ART
GALLERY

Yale University Art Gallery
Trip 1/30/13

York City Parks
Bienvenido a su parque. Este es un espacio público compartido que se ofrece para que lo disfrute y se recree. Los perros deben contar con las licencias y vacunas correspondientes. Sea cortés y respetuoso con los demás, y por favor mantenga limpio el parque.
Los reglamentos del parque prohíben:
• Botar basura y botar desechos
• Asar a la parrilla, excepto en áreas designadas
• Perros sin correa, excepto en las áreas designadas entre las 9pm-9am, cuando esté abierto el parque
• El uso de drogas ilegales y alcohol
• Alimentar a los pájaros y a las ardillas
• Ingresar al parque después de que ha cerrado
• Pedir y obstruir las entradas
• Amplificar sonidos, actuar y congregarse, realizar actividades comerciales, y vehículos, excepto con permiso
more information about Parks, please call 311 or visit www.nyc.gov/parks.
City of New York
Parks & Recreation
Michael R. Bloomberg, Mayor
Adrian Benepe, Commissioner
SATURDAY, MAY 4
FIRST STREET GREEN
www.firststreetgreenpark.org
New Museum's IDEAS CITY
First Park at 33 East 1st Street
Corner of Houston & 2nd Avenue

Jennifer Ewald / Jill Bunyea / Katerina Marcelja / Maura Whang / Ahmed Dirhalleh / Salvatore Cosenza / Corwin Carroll / Kasia Wilusz / Lyubov Tsinis / Benjamin Tulman / Brian Lantz / Nicholas Friedmann / Mohammed Tammam Munir / Adelaida Baez-Urena / Christina Hernandez / Paola Martinez / Ronald Martin / Bantwal Akshay Mallya / Alex la Ferla / Nagi Alamri / Nan Li / Nelly Sachakova / Michael Joseph

FACULTY: Bradley Horn / Elisabetta Terragni

THE CITY UNIVERSITY OF NEW YORK ADMINISTRATION

Matthew Goldstein
Chancellor

THE CITY COLLEGE OF NEW YORK CITY UNIVERSITY OF NEW YORK ADMINISTRATION

Lisa Staiano-Coico
President

Maurizio Trevisan
Provost

THE CITY COLLEGE OF NEW YORK BERNARD AND ANNE SPITZER SCHOOL OF ARCHITECTURE

George Ranalli
Dean

Peter Gisolfi
Professor, Chair

Gordon Gebert
Professor, Deputy Chair

Denise Hoffman-Brandt
Director,
Master of Landscape Architecture Program

Hillary Brown
Director,
Master of Sustainability Program

Bradley Horn
Director,
Master of Architecture Program

Michael Sorkin
Director,
Master of Urban Design Program

Evan Akselrad
Adjunct Professor

Venesa Alicea
Adjunct Professor

Jacob Alspector
Associate Professor

Robert Baker
Adjunct Professor

Nandini Bagchee
Assistant Professor

Thomas Beachdel
Adjunct Professor

Carmi Bee
Professor Emeritus

Marshall Berman*
Adjunct Professor

Michael Bobker
Adjunct Professor

Hillary Brown
Professor

Lance Jay Brown, FAIA
Professor

Sara Caples
Visiting Professor

Mi Tsung Chang
Assistant Professor

David Chapin
Adjunct Professor

Timothy Matthew Collins
Adjunct Professor

Caleb Crawford
Adjunct Professor

Yolande Daniels
Visiting Professor

Antonio Di Oronzo
Adjunct Professor

Johanna Dickson
Adjunct Professor

Alfred Eatman
Adjunct Professor

Jeremy Edmiston
Associate Professor

Jeffrey Feingold
Adjunct Professor

Alberto Foyo
Adjunct Professor

Isaac Gertman
Adjunct Professor

Burt Goncalves
Adjunct Professor

Domingo Gonzales
Adjunct Lecturer

Toni L. Griffin
Associate Professor

Marta Gutman
Associate Professor

Athanasios Haritos
Adjunct Professor

Daniel Hauben
Adjunct Lecturer

Adam Hayes
Adjunct Lecturer

Brian Healy
Visiting Professor

Ghislaine Hermanuz
Professor

Ali Hocek
Adjunct Professor

*Marshall Berman passed away in September 2013. He will be dearly missed at our School.

Leonard Hopper
Adjunct Professor

John Hong
Visiting Professor

Lewis Iglehart
Adjunct Professor

Marcha Johnson
Adjunct Professor

David Judelson
Adjunct Associate Professor

Vanessa Keith
Adjunct Professor

Joan Krevlin
Adjunct Professor

Andrew Lavallee
Adjunct Professor

Francis Leadon
Associate Professor

Amy Lerner
Adjunct Professor

Fabian Llonch
Associate Professor

Einat Manoff
Adjunct Professor

Audrey Matlock
Visiting Professor

W. Garrison McNeil
Professor Emeritus

Donald Mongitore
Adjunct Professor

John Murray
Adjunct Professor

Irma Ostroff
Adjunct Professor

Dominick Pilla
Associate Professor

Ivan Rosa
Adjunct Professor

Sandor Rosta
Adjunct Professor

James Russell
Adjunct Professor

Julio Salcedo-Fernandez
Associate Professor

Markus Schulte
Adjunct Professor

Catherine Seavitt-Nordenson
Associate Professor

Scott Shell
Adjunct Professor

Rebecca Siefert
Adjunct Lecturer

Morris Silberberg
Adjunct Professor

Brent Stringfellow
Adjunct Professor

Yehre Suh
Adjunct Professor

Joseph Tanney
Visiting Professor

Elisabetta Terragni
Associate Professor

Robert Twombly
Adjunct Professor

Albert Vecerka
Adjunct Associate Professor

Christian Volkmann
Associate Professor

Sean Weiss
Adjunct Lecturer

Lee Weintraub
Associate Professor

Barbara Wilks
Adjunct Associate Professor

June Williamson
Associate Professor

Suzan Wines
Adjunct Associate Professor

Andrew Zientek
Adjunct Professor

STAFF AND ADVISORS

Michael Miller
Director of Operations

Erica Torres
Executive Assistant to the Dean

Emily Ferrari
CUNY Office Assistant

Camille Hall
Director of Finance and Administration

Ghislaine Hermanuz
Professor,
Director of Advising

Alan Feigenberg
Advisor, Professor

Arnaldo Melendez
Advisor Undergraduate

Sara Morales
Graduate Advisor

Junko Fujimoto
Visual Resources Library Assistant

Carolina Colon
Assistant to the Chairperson

Judy Connorton
Architecture Librarian

Nilda Sanchez
Architecture Library Assistant

Jorge Plazas
Shop Director

Aja Garzon
Visual Resources Library Assitant

Esther Yang
Assistant Director of the J. Max Bond Center

Carolina Johnson Colon
Assistant to the Chair

CITY WORKS 7 STAFF

Nandini Bagchee
Co - Editor

Bradley Horn
Co - Editor

Salvatore Cosenza
Design / Production Coordinator

Jennifer Ewald
Design / Production Coordinator

BOOK CREDITS

Creative Direction by Leo Malinow
Graphic Design by Yanina Arabena
Copy Editing by Jorge Alvarez Spencer
Cover photograph by Albert Vecerka
Front flap photograph by Albert Vecerka
Back flap photograph by George Ranalli

Model photography by Salvatore Cosenza, Jennifer Ewald and the students of Spitzer School of Architecture.

ISBN 978-988-12252-7-6
Published by Oscar Riera Ojeda Publishers Limited
Printed in China by Artron Art Center

Oscar Riera Ojeda Publishers Limited
Unit 6, 22/Floor,
Far East Consortium Building,
121 Des Voeux Road Central, Hong Kong.
T: +852-5311-1625

Production Offices | China
Suit 19, Shenyun Road
Nanshan District, Shenzhen 518055
T:+86-755-8336-6138

www.oropublishers.com | www.oscarrieraojeda.com
contact us: oscar@oscarrieraojeda.com